SAAC

SIXTH EDITION

ULTIMATE

INTERVIEW

100s OF SAMPLE QUESTIONS AND ANSWERS FOR INTERVIEW SUCCESS

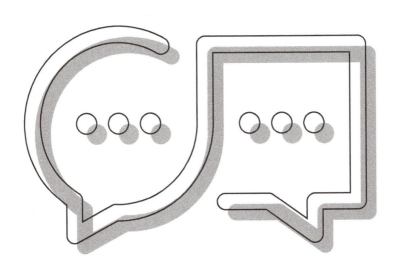

LYNN WILLI/

D0209224

MAR - - 2022

Publisher's note

Every possible effort has been made to ensure that the information contained in this book is accurate at the time of going to press, and the publishers and author cannot accept responsibility for any errors or omissions, however caused. No responsibility for loss or damage occasioned to any person acting, or refraining from action, as a result of the material in this publication can be accepted by the editor, the publishers or the author.

First published in Great Britain and the United States as *The Ultimate Interview Book* in 2005 by Kogan Page Limited
Second edition published in 2008 as *Ultimate Interview*
Third edition 2012
Fourth edition 2015
Fifth edition 2018
Sixth edition 2021

Apart from any fair dealing for the purposes of research or private study, or criticism or review, as permitted under the Copyright, Designs and Patents Act 1988, this publication may only be reproduced, stored or transmitted, in any form or by any means, with the prior permission in writing of the publishers, or in the case of reprographic reproduction in accordance with the terms and licences issued by the CLA. Enquiries concerning reproduction outside these terms should be sent to the publishers at the undermentioned addresses:

2nd Floor, 45 Gee Street	122 W 27th St, 10th Floor	4737/23 Ansari Road
London EC1V 3RS	New York, NY 10001	Daryaganj
United Kingdom	USA	New Delhi 110002
www.koganpage.com		India

Kogan Page books are printed on paper from sustainable forests.

© Carolyn Williamson, 2005, 2008, 2012, 2015, 2018, 2021

The right of Carolyn Williamson to be identified as the author of this work has been asserted by her in accordance with the Copyright, Designs and Patents Act 1988.

ISBNs

Hardback	978 1 39860 215 1
Paperback	978 1 39860 213 7
Ebook	978 1 39860 214 4

British Library Cataloguing-in-Publication Data

A CIP record for this book is available from the British Library.

Library of Congress Control Number

2021939391

Typeset by Integra Software Services, Pondicherry
Print production managed by Jellyfish
Printed and bound by CPI Group (UK) Ltd, Croydon, CR0 4YY

CONTENTS

Introduction   1

1   **Know your enemy**   3
Understanding interviewers
What do they want?   3
What sort of things are they looking for?   4
What will happen at the interview?   5
What sort of questions will they ask?   6
How do they know what they're looking for?   7

2   **Prepare yourself**   10
What you need to know before the interview
What should you prepare?   11
Exhibit 1: Evidence that you meet their needs   11
Exhibit 2: Reassuring answers and explanations   14
Exhibit 3: Industry knowledge   16
Exhibit 4: The reasons you want this job   19

3   **Standing out**   21
How to be an outstanding candidate
Why are these qualities so important?   22

4   **Answering questions**   31
What the interviewer will ask and what you need to tell them
Make a good impression   31
Three cardinal rules   36

5   **Starting the interview**   38
What to expect from the interview and how to begin confidently

6   **Questions they ask everybody**   44
Standard questions you should prepare for

7 Behavioural questions 52
Some questions dig deeper than others
What are the important points? 53

8 Questions for practical jobs 57
Core question, 'Are you reliable?'
Professional knowledge 66

9 Questions for creative jobs 68
Core question, 'Will you deliver?'
Professional knowledge 79

10 Questions for clerical and administrative jobs 81
Core question, 'Are you efficient?'
Professional knowledge 92

11 Questions for sales and marketing jobs 94
Core question, 'Can you sell?'
Professional knowledge 106

12 Questions for technical jobs 108
Core question, 'Can you do the job?'
Professional knowledge 121

13 Questions for management jobs 124
Core question, 'Will you get results?'
Professional knowledge 144

14 Questions for customer relations jobs 146
Core question, 'Are you customer focused?'
Professional knowledge 154

15 Questions for school and college leavers 156
What to do if you don't have experience
Transferable skills 157
Professional knowledge 166

16 Tackling the difficult questions 168
Handling questions about perceived areas of weakness
Inappropriate and illegal questions 175

17 Dealing with tricky questions 178

What to say when there's no clear answer

Dealing with critical or negative questions 178

Questions about salary 183

Answering closed questions 185

18 Answering off-the-wall questions 188

What is the interviewer really asking?

Questions asking you to work something out 189

'Psychological' questions 190

19 Your questions for the interviewer 193

What to ask at the end of the interview

20 Variations on the theme 197

Different types of interview and how to deal with them confidently

Screening interviews 197

Telephone interviews 198

Video interviews 199

Panel interviews 200

Serial interviews 201

Assessment centres 202

Informal interviews 203

Second interviews 203

21 The interview: Future trends 205

Tasks and tests that are already in use and how to prepare for them

The interview – future trends 205

Making a presentation 206

Showing your portfolio 207

Technical and attainment tests 207

Physical tests 208

Job-replica exercises 208

Group exercises 209

Psychometric tests 210

Future possibilities 216

22 Looking the part   219
Making a good impression from the start
Appearance   219
Behaviour   221
Overcoming nerves   223

23 What happens next?   227
What to do after the interview
While you're waiting for their decision   227
If they don't make you an offer   228
If they do make you an offer   233

24 Interviews in a nutshell   236
The three essential questions you need to know about
Main Question 1: Can you do the job?   236
Main Question 2: Will you do the job?   237
Main Question 3: Will you fit in?   238

Index to the questions   239
Index   247

INTRODUCTION

Congratulations! You've got an interview. This is meant to be good news, so why do you feel as if you've just had advance notice of your execution?

Don't worry, you *should* feel nervous. It's natural. Interviews are very important; they stand between you and the job of your dreams, or at least an honest job with a reasonable salary. And it's possible that, with jobs in rather short supply recently, this interview is a long-anticipated event. Feel nervous for the right reasons, though. Actors about to go on stage can feel tense because of two things. Either they don't know their lines, haven't rehearsed, don't know what to expect and are afraid of making a fool of themselves; or they're fully prepared and anxious to give their very best performance. The first sort of nerves makes you feel sick and hinders your delivery; the second sort gives you the extra pizzazz you need for a winning presentation.

Now, more than ever before, you need to do everything you can to get the winning edge. So how do you turn the first sort of nerves into the second sort? Like the good actor, you prepare thoroughly beforehand.

Preparing for an interview isn't difficult, but it does take time and effort. The two big things you need to know, and know thoroughly, are: what they want; and what you've got. Sort those out, match them up, put them across convincingly and you can't go far wrong. The rest of this book tells you how to do just that, along with some other important points to help you get ready.

Don't wait until the morning of the interview to read this book and find out how to prepare. Do it now and do it thoroughly. Not only will it take a lot of the pressure off you, but it will give you the chance to prepare really good answers and rehearse them exhaustively. When you know what to expect and how to handle it, you'll feel completely confident when you go in front of your live audience – the interviewer.

Ah, the interviewer. Let's scotch a few myths about interviewers:

They are not out to humiliate you.

They will not ask you trick questions for no reason.

They will not seek out your weak spots and exploit them.

If they didn't think you could do the job, they wouldn't have asked you to the interview.

There are no preferred candidates; everyone is on an equal footing.

They never ask people to interviews just to make up the numbers.

Interviewers try their very best to be impartial. However, every interviewer is an individual with individual preferences and biases. Different people put a different emphasis on different things. Some will be influenced by a confident delivery, some by a striking first impression, and others prefer someone who takes time to think things through.

What they have in common is that they all, believe it or not, want you to do your best and will go to great lengths to see that you do – preparing the questions, arranging the interview room, putting you at your ease. What all interviewers want is someone who can do the job. When you walk in the door, they hope it's going to be you. Your task is to convince them that they're right.

At the end of each chapter, you'll find quotes from the people who actually do the interviewing. This is advice straight from the horse's mouth – if they'll excuse the expression. This is what interviewers actually think and feel, and what they wish they could tell their interviewees before the interview. Look at what these experts have to say, take note of what they want, and there's an excellent chance that you'll soon find yourself being offered the job of your dreams.

KNOW YOUR ENEMY
UNDERSTANDING INTERVIEWERS

Before you prepare for the interview, it's useful to understand how most organi-zations decide what they are looking for in a candidate, and how they use this to choose the questions they ask at the interview. It can also be helpful to know how the selection procedure works, why employers conduct interviews and what's likely to happen at the average interview.

What do they want?

Employers want:

someone who *can* do the job, ie someone who has:

- the experience;
- the knowledge;
- the skills;

someone who *will* do the job, ie someone who has:

- the personal characteristics;
- the enthusiasm and commitment;

Contact the company

The first thing most people do is go to the company's web page. There is more information about all the things you *could* find out later in this chapter, but at the very least there are three important things that you definitely need to know about any company or organization before you go for an interview with them:

1   A broad idea of the company's culture, mission and values. You should be able to pick this up throughout the site from the home page onwards, but especially on the 'About' page on which the company literally, and very usefully, tells you about itself, so pay particular attention to this one.

2   Current company news. Always look at recent news on the company's press page at the very least. For more news you can also enter the company name into a search engine and see if it crops up in any articles, or you can sign up for specific alerts from the search engine that will let you know about any new press postings.

3   The key company members. Names are useful, but photographs and, even better, a short biography will help transform them into real people in your mind.

As well as the company website, you can also look for background information on your chosen area in news groups, interest groups and chat groups, and on professional organization, as well as making use of professionally focused social media websites.

By the time you get as far as an interview, your prospective employer already knows the specific details of what they are looking for – we'll look at how later. Having read your CV or application form, they also know how well you match their profile. If they are interviewing you, you can be sure you're a good match.

The purpose of the interview, then, is to probe more fully into those key areas. They need to:

check you have the relevant skills and experience stated in your CV;

clarify any puzzling, missing or less than favourable features;

complete the picture of you presented by your CV.

What sort of things are they looking for?

While they are sorting and grading the CVs and application forms, employers initially look for clear evidence of:

essential skills, qualifications, abilities and achievements;

desirable skills, qualifications, abilities and achievements;

industry knowledge;

career development;

consistency and stability of employment within the industry, including previous employers;

general employment stability, including average period in any one job.

At the interview they will be trying to confirm that you have all of the above and to fill in the details by probing your background and experience face to face. They are also looking for those harder-to-define skills and personal attributes that will ensure that you fit comfortably into the organization, and will be a useful member of the team and an asset to the company.

What will happen at the interview?

Most interviewers these days try to ensure the interview follows the same course for each candidate, so most interviews follow the same basic structure:

The welcome. An introduction designed to put you at your ease, which often includes a general greeting and brief chat – *'Thank you for coming,' 'Did you have a good journey?'* and so on – followed by an outline of the interview and a brief account of the job and the company.

The questions. The interviewer will often start the main part of the interview by asking you an open question such as *'Would you give me a rundown of your current post?'* or *'Would you describe your current responsibilities to me?'* The purpose of this is to see how you apply your knowledge, skills and abilities in your current job. They will then go on to ask a set of standard structured questions they are asking every applicant.

If there are things on your CV they want to look at more closely – an unusual career path or gaps in your employment history – they will also ask you about these. Unlike the structured questions, these are person-specific and will be different for each interviewee.

Both sets of questions usually follow a logical structure and an orderly sequence. However, towards the end, the interviewer may find they want more information about something covered earlier, or they may want to go back and enquire into something in more depth, so don't be surprised if the interviewer appears to revert to an earlier question.

Over to you. When the interviewer is happy they've got all the information they want, they'll ask if you have any questions yourself.

The finish. The interviewer will usually conclude the interview by describing what will happen next – whether there will be any further stage in the interview process (a second interview, assessments or tests, etc), when you might expect to hear the outcome, whether they will ring or write to you with their decision. If they are offering travel expenses, they will usually explain what to do at this stage. They will end by thanking you for coming to the interview and wishing you well.

What sort of questions will they ask?

As we've seen above, most interviewers prepare two sets of questions: standard, structured questions; and person-specific questions.

The structured questions will be the same for all candidates and are usually compiled well in advance of the interview. They are based on a job description and a person specification – more about these later – and are designed to probe how well each applicant matches the criteria for that specific job. They include questions such as: *'What do you see as the main priorities of this particular job?' 'How would you deal with an aggressive client?' 'Tell me about an occasion when you had to motivate a team member. How did you go about it?'* and *'Where do you see this industry expanding in the next five years?'* They want to see if you have the abilities required to do the job.

Structured questions make the interview process fair because each applicant is matched against the requirements of the job rather than being rated against each other.

Person-specific questions are designed to explore your particular circumstances more fully and are based on your CV or application form. These questions often seek out and expose your weak spots: *'How well do you think you will settle down to a 9-to-5 job after extensive travelling?' 'Do you feel that this job might be a bit of a step down for you?' 'Unlike your current job, this job involves a great deal of contact with the public. How do you think you would handle that?'* and *'Why are you considering leaving your current job after only six months?'*

This is often seen as the 'sticky' bit of the interview, but looked at positively, it's actually your opportunity to reassure the interviewer and set their mind at rest. We'll look at how to do this in great detail later in Chapter 15, Tackling the difficult questions.

On the whole, the interviewer will want to investigate anything they pick up from your CV or application form that suggests:

an unusual career path;

frequent job changes and/or gaps in employment;

a lack of relevant qualifications or training;

a lack of relevant background or experience;

unclear personal attributes or specific aptitudes.

Both sets of questions can, to a large extent, be anticipated, and we'll look at exactly how to do that and prepare for the interview in Chapter 2.

How do they know what they're looking for?

Before advertising the job, the employer, or the human resources department in larger organizations, will have compiled two documents: the job description; and the person specification.

The job description gives an overview of the key elements of the job, including:

the job title;

grade;

location;

a summary of the tasks involved;

responsibilities;

key skills;

result criteria – for example, producing x number of item y to quality z;

essential qualifications needed;

who the job holder reports to;

level of authority.

The person specification is a more subjective document outlining the skills, abilities, characteristics and behaviour needed to carry out the job successfully, with each element rated as either essential or desirable. It often includes:

Education and training:
  - level of general qualifications;
  - specific professional qualifications;
  - job-related training.

Knowledge and experience:
  - job-related knowledge and experience;
  - general experience;
  - technical skills;
  - special skills: languages, IT skills, etc.

Specific aptitudes:
  - any special criteria for the job, such as verbal or written language aptitude;
  - creativity, ability to work with numbers, manual dexterity, etc.

Disposition:

- characteristics: initiative, motivation, resilience, etc;
- working style: leadership ability, team-working skills, etc;
- competencies: problem-solving skills, ability to plan and prioritize, etc.

Interpersonal skills:

- communication skills;
- management and team-building skills;
- rapport-building skills: customer service skills, influencing skills, etc.

Special considerations:

- any special circumstances specific to the job – ability to live in, ability to travel, being on call, shift pattern availability, etc.

These two documents will be used to draw up the job advertisement. They may also be used to compile the application form, and they will almost certainly be used to compare, rate and rank applicants. They will, ultimately, be used to decide which key areas the structured questions at the interview will cover and will form the basis for the questions you will be asked.

As CVs or application forms come in, they are given a brief initial read-through and those meeting the basic requirements go on to a more thorough screening to select people for interview.

Table 1.1 shows one way of selecting applicants for interview – it's a section from what's called a comparison matrix, matching applicants against the person specification.

As CVs or application forms are scrutinized, the information is entered on the matrix to see how well it fits. The six applicants with the best match will be called for interview, the next six best will be kept in reserve in case any of the first choice can't come, and the rest will probably be sent a rejection letter.

TABLE 1.1 Matching applicants against the person specification

Applicant	Training and Education			Knowledge and Experience			Specific Aptitudes			Disposition		
	1	2	3	1	2	3	1	2	3	1	2	3
Paul Atkins		✔				✔		✔		✔		
Helen Brown			✔			✔		✔				✔
John Dean	✔					✔			✔			✔
Carol Dyer			✔		✔			✔			✔	

Grade 1: fair; 2: good; 3: excellent

As you can see from Table 1.1, a matrix helps to make information clear, even if the decisions aren't always clear cut. Paul Atkins, for example, has excellent knowledge and experience, but his specific abilities are less good, and his disposition is only fair. He probably wouldn't reach the interview stage.

In contrast, while John Dean's education and training are only fair, he has excellent experience, the specific aptitudes required and an excellent disposition for the job. Depending on how much weight the employer gives to education, and the reasons for his lack of formal training, John Dean has an excellent chance of being interviewed, where he will probably be asked person-specific questions about his educational background.

Now that you know how interviewers prepare interviews, let's look at how you can use this information to prepare for your own interview.

KEY TAKEAWAYS FROM CHAPTER 1

Knowing how interviews work helps you to deal with them confidently.

- Understanding how companies decide what they are looking for in a candidate, and how they build the interview around that, will help you to prepare for it.

- Understanding the basic structure of the interview means you can anticipate what's likely to happen and plan accordingly.

- Researching the company will always give you information you can use to prepare great answers.

WHAT THE EXPERT SAYS

I've had 20 years' experience in human resources. During that time I've seen it move away from very formal interviews to more relaxed informal ones. There's no point putting people on the spot or intimidating them; we want them to relax and be at their best. You get more out of people when they feel at ease, and you can make a more accurate assessment when you can see the natural person.

Gail Milne, HR Manager, Teddington Controls

2

PREPARE YOURSELF
WHAT YOU NEED TO KNOW BEFORE THE INTERVIEW

Now that you know how the interviewer prepares the interview, you can begin to understand what they want to know and to anticipate what questions they'll ask. You know that:

They have a job description and a person specification.

They read your CV or application form to see how well you match.

Therefore, you can expect that:

They'll ask searching questions about all the skills, qualifications and personal qualities mentioned in the job advertisement and the job description.

They'll probe those areas of your CV where the match is less good or less clear.

As well as that, they will expect you to know something about the organization and the job you're applying for, and to be able to offer convincing reasons why you want the job.

Make sure that:

- you understand what skills, qualities and experience are required to do the job;
- you know what skills, qualities and experience you have that match those requirements;
- you can give examples of how, when and where you've demonstrated those skills and qualities;
- you can present those examples concisely and confidently.

What should you prepare?

As you can see from the information above, preparing for interviews is actually quite straightforward in theory, if quite demanding in practice. You need to present your case clearly. Like a top-rank lawyer presenting a case in court, you need to have your 'exhibits' ready:

Exhibit 1: evidence that you meet their needs with regard to skills, qualities and experience;

Exhibit 2: reassuring answers and satisfactory explanations for those areas of your CV where you don't quite match or where there might be some other problem;

Exhibit 3: some knowledge of the industry or business sector, and the interviewing company in particular;

Exhibit 4: sound reasons why you are applying for the job.

Let's look at each of these in more detail.

Exhibit 1: Evidence that you meet their needs

This will form the major part of the interview, so how do you set about preparing evidence that will convince them? You need examples of occasions when you've successfully displayed your skills and qualities and which demonstrate your areas of experience. These are known collectively as your competencies – the things you're competent doing because you've done them before.

Reread the job posting and the job description

The first and most obvious thing to do is to reread the original job advertisement. Next, take a look at any information that accompanies the application form. There's usually a detailed job description, and some companies post quite comprehensive information. If you don't have enough, look on their website or contact the company to see if there are any additional details about the job you could use. Add any specific requirements to your list. The more information you have, the more thoroughly you can prepare.

Study the information carefully. You must make absolutely sure that you know exactly what the job entails; and that you know exactly what skills, qualities, experience and qualifications are required.

Find examples

Once you know what they want, you need to review what you've got. Make sure that:

> you have the skills and qualities required;
>
> you can give examples of how, when and where you've demonstrated them in the past;
>
> you can present those examples confidently and enthusiastically.

Go about this systematically and actually write things down. It's easy to think to yourself, 'Oh, I've done this' or 'Yes, I can do that.' What you are looking for, and what you will have to present to the interviewer, is *evidence*.

> Work through the job ad and job description (and any other relevant information), underlining the key points:
>
> - specific skills;
> - areas of experience;
> - responsibilities;
> - qualifications and training;
> - knowledge areas;
> - qualities and characteristics;
> - abilities.
>
> Make a list of all the requirements.
>
> Make notes that show how, when and where you've had experience of each requirement. Think of examples from:
>
> - your current job;
> - previous jobs;
> - unpaid positions: voluntary work, community associations, organizations and sports teams;
> - your personal life.
>
> Study your notes and jot down the details of specific occasions that show you using each particular competency. For example, the ad asks for someone who is calm under pressure. You note down the occasion when an order had to be completed in half the usual time along with details of how you kept calm, organized yourself and prioritized the workload so you could meet the deadline, saving the company a large penalty charge.
>
> Sort and polish your notes until you have at least one good example for each requirement.

If you ever watch chat shows, you'll recognize that some people interview well and others don't. The worst people either give one-word answers or else go on at great length to no particular point. The best people offer interesting, concise anecdotes that answer the question and expand on it to good effect.

Turn your basic information into anecdotes that give the interviewer the full story. For example, if they ask *'How would you cope with an aggressive customer?'* rather than say just 'I would do x, y and z', give them an anecdote to show how you actually dealt tactfully and successfully with an aggressive customer in a real-life situation.

Arm yourself with as many of these stories as are relevant to the job in question. Polish them until you are certain they reflect your true abilities.

Bring benefits

Employers particularly like to know that the person they're employing will be of benefit to the company. It's very important, therefore, to prepare examples and anecdotes about the occasions when you:

increased:

- profits;
- production;
- turnover;
- sales;
- efficiency;
- market opportunity.

decreased:

- staff turnover or absenteeism.
- risk;
- the time taken to do something or process something;
- potential problems;
- costs;
- waste.

improved:

- competitive advantage;
- marketability;
- organization;
- information flow or communication;
- staff performance;
- teamwork and staff relationships.

Practise

Memorize these answers and practise delivering them until you feel comfortable and at ease. Nerves are guaranteed to make you forgetful, so, like an actor learning lines, rehearse your key answers until they come easily to you. Role-play them with a friend or colleague if possible, so you get used to telling your anecdotes to an audience.

Exhibit 2: Reassuring answers and explanations

Few people exactly match the job description, but remember that you must come pretty close or they wouldn't be interviewing you. You may need to answer a few nagging doubts, however, and being prepared will make it a lot easier.

Look at your CV or application form with an employer's eye and match it to the job description and job ad. Are there any obvious mismatches such as:

shortage of relevant skills or experience;

shortage of experience in certain areas;

lack of qualifications.

You can be certain that you will be questioned about these inconsistencies. There's no reason to be worried by questions about these things if, as above, you prepare your evidence before the interview and can put their mind at rest.

We will be looking at these issues in much greater depth in Chapter 16, Tackling the difficult questions, so don't let them worry you too much. Many people find this aspect of the interview intimidating; indeed, some find it puts them off even applying for jobs in case they are asked questions about difficult areas of their career history. Employers are often much more flexible than you think, and if they have asked you to an interview, they are willing to be convinced.

Briefly:

If you have simply missed skills or experience off your CV not knowing they were relevant, simply reply positively with good back-up anecdotes to demonstrate your knowledge.

If you genuinely lack workplace experience in a particular area, they are possibly right to worry about how you will manage when faced with it at work. Your best way to reassure them is to find the nearest experience you have to it – either from work or from outside interests or voluntary work – and show, with appropriate anecdotes, how you coped then and how you relate this to your future role.

If you lack qualifications or training, does your practical experience make up for this? If so, explain how. Many older people, for example, manage very well having been promoted into jobs that would demand a degree from a new starter.

Are you currently undergoing training or education that will fill a particular gap? Or are you willing to train, possibly in your own time or at your own expense, to remedy the situation? Again, it would help to offer an anecdote about how quickly you've picked things up in the past, or how well you managed to work and train at the same time before.

The other thing to look for on your CV or application form is anything that suggests you've had problems with employment in the past. In the interviewer's mind, this means:

any gaps in employment;

frequent job changes;

moves backwards or sideways;

abrupt career changes;

inconsistent choices of work.

If any of these things leap out from your CV, you should seriously look at giving it a revamp. However, it can't be too bad or they wouldn't be interviewing you. You still have to answer their worries, though, and, as above, we will be looking at this in great detail in Chapter 15, Tackling the difficult questions.

Have your story ready. You can't lie outright, but you can think about how to present any problems in the best possible light and prepare your answers accordingly.

You may have very good reasons for employment gaps or job changes. If so, explain them clearly. If, for example, you have a year-long gap because of travel, explain this and offer a brief anecdote focusing on what you learnt during that time that will be relevant to the job – how you got on with people from all walks of life or coped with potential disaster, for example. You also need to make it clear that the travel bug, or whatever caused the gap, is out of your system now, and you won't be disappearing from this job at a moment's notice.

If you have no good reasons, just explain any contributing factors without sounding as if you are making excuses for yourself. What you *must* do in this case is emphasize that you are a very different person now, and give them anecdotes to back this up. Describe how you've now found your true niche in life, how you stuck to your last job despite difficulties, how you overcame something that would formerly have made you leave, etc.

Exhibit 3: Industry knowledge

We've already looked at how important getting a detailed job description is, and how useful it is for preparing your interview answers. The next most important information you need is anything about the industry and, specifically, the company doing the interviewing.

Imagine going on a date with someone who says they've always longed to meet you, are absolutely fascinated by you and are really enthusiastic about future dates. Yet, when you question them, they know absolutely nothing about you and don't seem particularly interested in finding out, either. Would you think them genuine, or a total sham? Well, companies can be just as sensitive.

The more senior the position, the more they'll expect you to know, but at any level industry knowledge wins you gold stars at interview. A good grounding in company background also helps your confidence and enhances your performance.

How do you find out?

Someone who will fit in, ie someone who:

- – understands and appreciates the company's culture – its values and purpose;
- – works well with colleagues;
- – takes instructions, suggestions and criticism constructively.

You can always ring the company and ask for information. You don't have to pretend to be an investor or a customer; just explain that you have an interview and you'd like some information about the organization to read beforehand. You should fairly easily be able to get hold of:

sales, marketing and advertising brochures;

the annual report;

any customer newsletter or magazine;

any in-house staff newsletter.

Business journals and trade publications

Trade and business directories will give you information about specific companies, from how long they've been going to the number of people they employ.

Every industry and virtually every type of job has its own newspaper or journal that will tell you what is happening in that particular sector. If you don't know about the ones in your field, there are online directories for trade-related journals and publications that will help you find them. They can tell you about professional or trade associations that are relevant to you and that will also have useful information. They'll also tell you about interesting and useful websites that could give you more information.

People

Do you have friends, current or former colleagues, or business contacts with information about the company or industry, or can you get to meet people through them? Informal inside information is valuable and would definitely increase your confidence. Without digging for company secrets or gossip, insider knowledge can help you gauge the company culture and direction as well as giving you an employee-eye view of the organization.

People who have business contacts with the company could also provide information, so always nurture good relationships with customers, suppliers, representatives, sales people, etc when you get the opportunity.

Use your library

One of the best places to start looking for information is your public library. It will, of course, have full internet access available for your online research, and you should be able to find many of the directories, journals and other publications mentioned above. It will also be able to help you find out about professional associations and other organizations that could be useful to you, such as local business groups where you can network.

What are you looking for?

While you are gathering all this information, what are you actually looking for? What do you need to know?

Apart from getting a general feel for the company and some idea of the corporate culture, background and direction, some specific questions you might want answered are:

What does the company do?
- What are the company's products and/or services?
- What is its profile in the marketplace? How does it like to be seen?
- How and where are goods or services produced?
- How are they provided or distributed?

Who does it do it for?
- What is the market for these goods or services?
- Who are the actual customers?

- Is the market expanding or contracting?
- What are they doing about it in either case?

How is it organized?

- How big is the company?
- Is it a single company or a conglomerate?
- Are they multinational?
- Are there lots of subsidiaries and divisions, or is everything centralized?
- How is your particular part of it structured?

What's the competition?

- Who are its competitors?
- What are they currently doing?
- How does it position itself against them?

What's its history?

- Where did it come from, when was it established, how did it start out and how was it built up?
- What are its biggest achievements?
- Was it bigger or smaller in the past?
- Is the area you are entering increasing or decreasing in size, prestige, etc?
- Have there been takeovers, mergers, buyouts, downsizing?
- What has changed radically over the years?

What's its future?

- What is the company's vision? Does it have a mission statement, for example?
- What are the current priorities?
- What are its prospects?
- What are its major current and future projects (as far as you can legitimately find out)?
- What is the biggest threat currently facing the company and/or the industry as a whole?
- What is the greatest opportunity confronting it?

Although these sound like very detailed questions, they are the sort of thing you can pick up quite easily and which will quickly build into a clear picture of the place where you are hoping to work.

The level of detail you will want to go into depends on the type of job and the level of seniority you are applying for. An executive, for example, would need to demonstrate a high degree of company and industry knowledge. But even if you are only applying for the most junior job on the lowest rung of the hierarchy, you should have a clear idea of at least what the company does and whom it does it for.

There is also another very good reason for gathering this information, one that could give you the winning edge you need, that we will come to in Chapter 3.

Exhibit 4: The reasons you want this job

Well, why *do* you want this job?

Don't be vague about your reasons. You need to have a clear idea of how this position fits in with your career progression and overall goals. Above all, you need to show how well you fit the job profile, and how this post is a natural progression from your current job. You need, in other words, to show that this job could have been made for you or, from the employer's point of view, that you could have been made for the job.

Think in terms of what you can bring to the job, rather than what you can get from it. It does no harm to prepare and rehearse an answer, showing how the job:

matches your skills and abilities;

follows naturally from your existing experience;

gives you the chance to use those skills and talents for the company's benefit;

presents you with challenges you have the background and experience to tackle successfully;

gives you the opportunity to play a key role in an organization or industry you respect.

You now have a fully prepared case for your suitability with all your evidence at your fingertips, ready to bring into play at every opportunity during the interview. You know exactly what skills and experience are required to do the job; you know how your own skills and experience fit those requirements; you can give concrete examples of when and where you've demonstrated those skills, and when it comes to those areas where you might not be such a good fit, you are prepared with reassuring answers for the interviewer. But there's still something more you can do – something that could be just what you need to make you stand out and give you that winning edge. That's what we'll look at in the next chapter.

KEY TAKEAWAYS FROM CHAPTER 2

The interviewer is thoroughly prepared - you should be, too:

- Have your evidence ready and well rehearsed before you go into the interview.
- Rather than just saying you can do X, Y or Z, offer real-life examples of a time you successfully did it.
- Know what benefits you have brought to previous employers, and what you will bring to this one.
- Know where your weak spots are and prepare accordingly.
- Know why you want the job and how it fits with your goals.
- Don't try to work in the dark. The more you know about the company, the better you can prepare your answers.

WHAT THE EXPERT SAYS

Prepare. Do some background research on the job and the company. We send out an information pack which includes the job description and the person specification. People coming to an interview should at least have read that. It shows some interest and enthusiasm.

Gail Milne, HR Manager, Teddington Controls

WHAT THE EXPERT SAYS

Do your preparation and make sure you know what the job entails. Read the advert and the job description word for word; all the key points are made in there. Match your skills and experience to the job's needs; don't make the interviewer do all the work. I'm afraid no preparation often means no job.

Tina M Buchanan, Group HR Director, Hamworthy Combustion Engineering

3

STANDING OUT
HOW TO BE AN OUTSTANDING CANDIDATE

Up until now, our focus has been very much on demonstrating the skills and competencies needed for the job. However, while these are of paramount importance, when employers can choose their new employee from a pool of equally qualified interviewees, how can you make sure that *you* stand out?

Organizations increasingly want more from candidates. As competition for jobs in all sectors intensifies, what the employer looks for is a guarantee that the candidate will actually deliver what their CV promises.

The question today isn't 'Can you do the job?' but, '*Will* you do the job?'

What they are looking for is evidence of 'employability', and employability is different from your qualifications, skills and experience, it's about your attitude, behaviour and personal qualities. The highly employable candidate offers more than a list of skills and workplace experience – they can also demonstrate that they are a dependable team player and will be a fully contributing member of the organization they are joining.

First of all, understand the importance to organizations of:

- **contribution** – your willingness to give that bit extra, to make a difference
- **cultural fit** – your appreciation of the aims and values of the organization, to care about what they care about
- **motivation** – your energy, drive and ambition on behalf of yourself, your team, and the organization as a whole
- **engagement** – your willingness to take on responsibility, to meet people, problems and opportunities more than half way

This is what businesses want from all their employees – from the head of the board to the lowliest shelf-stacker. These are the things that make sure that businesses are successful – that organizations grow and thrive and that every-body stays employed. Most companies survive on the tightest margins these days and their biggest asset has to be their staff.

To this end, employers look for the personal qualities in their staff that they know will best guarantee they can deliver these requirements. These personal qualities are:

- **intelligence** – curiosity, common sense, and practicality
- **likeability** – warmth, friendliness, agreeableness, co-operation and a degree of emotional intelligence
- **competence** – responsibility, initiative, reliability and dependability
- **integrity** – honesty, openness, scrupulousness, congruence
- **positivity** – energy, pro-activity, confidence, a 'can do' attitude
- **adaptability** – flexibility, the ability to grow and change to meet demands

Why are these qualities so important?

Intelligence

We're not talking about super-braininess here, just the ability to use common sense and engage with problems and opportunities rather than taking a 'don't know, don't care' attitude. People who apply their intelligence to their job have the curiosity to find out what's needed; the common sense to understand why it's important; and the practicality to act on it. People who trust their intelligence are confident about what they undertake – they can analyse situations accurately and make informed choices, and they have the ability to make quick decisions and take appropriate action. They are also willing to learn and to use what they have learnt to try new approaches to problems. This means they remain motivated and engaged, and often make a significant contribution to any organization they belong to.

Likeability

Most work is done in teams and if the teams don't work well together it can mean big problems for the company. Similarly, many jobs are customer or client focused, whether that means external clients such as the public, or inter-nal clients such as another department. Poor client interactions can spell dis-aster. People with good 'likeability skills' – interpersonal and communication skills – are essential. They are agreeable, co-operative, supportive and socia-ble and they contribute to the successful operation of their team, department and, ultimately, the company. Their interpersonal connections also hold the company together and ensure that it remains a cohesive unit. They are instrumental to maintaining the company culture.

Competence

The importance of this quality almost goes without saying. Someone who is competent makes sure every task they undertake is completed thoroughly, capably and to the best of their ability. They take responsibility for ensuring that everything goes well and can be relied on to deliver what is needed when it's needed. It's not just a matter of having the technical skills to deliver this sort of service; it's having the attitude and will to do so that's important as well.

Integrity

Companies have to trust their personnel. An organization where mistrust and suspicion abounds is rarely a thriving, successful one. The company culture will be too stagnant and de-motivating to work – teams can't thrive where members don't trust each other, and departments don't work when managers are continually checking up on their staff. Similarly, the public, clients and customers have to have faith in the company – that it will deal with them honestly and behave with integrity – now more than ever before. The slightest hint of dishonesty or double-dealing in any company operating today and it will start to haemorrhage clients immediately. So the company is fundamentally reliant on the honesty and integrity of the people it employs if all its staff are to remain motivated and engaged or, indeed, employed.

Positivity

Positive people are better to work with. They aren't just happier and more cheerful to have around; they perform better too, bringing passion and enthusiasm to the job. Because they expect positive results, they are willing to go the extra mile to achieve them and more likely to persist in the face of obstacles. Their ability to make the best of things and to see the good in people and situations turns challenges into opportunities. Even better, positive attitudes tend to be catching and positive people can inspire and motivate others – which is great because positivity engenders creativity and fresh ideas which is what businesses rely on in order to thrive.

Adaptability

Change in the workplace is normal. With continuous changes in technology, business practice, markets, economies and society in general, companies need people who are adaptable and open to learning new methods, taking on new responsibilities, finding ways around obstacles and generally responding positively to fluctuating circumstances. They depend on employees being able to shift priorities and bounce back – to look for ways to make change work rather than complain that it won't. From being flexible enough to handle the daily give-and-take required for working in a team, to responding with energy and poise to major crises, adaptable people contribute to the continuing success of the organization as it evolves to meet new circumstances.

Showing your qualities

As you did with your skills and experience, think about how, when and where you have demonstrated these qualities because it's important that you go to the interview armed with this evidence of your employability. It's not sufficient to simply reiterate your skills and qualifications. The interviewer already knows you have most of the necessary competencies — that's why they're interviewing you. One of the main reasons they now want to meet you in person is to gauge your personal attributes and attitudes and see whether your skills are underpinned by the sort of qualities that can be of use in the job and which will make you an asset to the organization. You need to demonstrate them just as thoroughly at the interview as you would any of your other workplace skills and experience.

Imagine, for example, a well-qualified candidate who perfectly matches the job description and who goes to the interview fully prepared to talk about his skills and qualifications. He feels he has done well in the interview and is bewildered not to be offered the job. This happens not once but several times.

Eventually he interviews with a company that offers feedback and they tell him that while they had been impressed by his skills and experience, they felt he came across as reserved and un-engaged, even a bit superior. He realizes he has been so focused on getting his skills across and being a perfect match, he has come over as being a bit of an automaton – all work and no personality. Employers are worried about his ability to fit in, get on with his colleagues and work as part of a team.

He gives more thought to demonstrating his personal qualities and focuses on his likeability and positivity. At his next interview he relaxes, smiles more and is warmer and more friendly towards the interviewer – much more his natural self. As well as that, he expresses more of an interest in the company and the work of the department, asking relevant questions and bringing more of his knowledge about the company culture and values into his responses. He also emphasizes his role working as part of a team in a couple of his answers, showing how he contributed to their success rather than focusing on his personal performance alone. The result is much more positive and it isn't long before he lands a job.

Another candidate has outstanding academic qualifications and looks really good on paper. When it comes to the interview, however, it's clear that she expects those qualifications to do all the work. She knows it's perfectly obvious that she can do the job, but she doesn't understand that there is no evidence that she *will* do the job – that she will work comfortably with others towards a common goal, use her undoubted intelligence for practical ends, see the value of ensuring that all the little things go well, adapt graciously when the client changes the brief, and bounce back when her ideas are rejected. The interviewer would like to employ her but just can't take the risk – the job goes to a less academic but more employable interviewee who goes out of her way to demonstrate her positive, agreeable, competent 'can-do' attitude to the job.

Demonstrate your cultural fit

Steve Jobs, former CEO of Apple Computer Inc, said: 'Find people who are competent and really bright, but more importantly, find people who care about exactly the same things you care about.' Having seen the success of Apple, more and more employers are following his way of thinking.

Do your research – find out what the company interviewing you cares about. If the website mentions customer service in every paragraph, that's a very strong clue. What are the skills and personal qualities needed for first rate customer service? You may have a CV containing four pages of customer service experience, but how are you going to demonstrate in the actual interview that you are someone customers like and trust? By being a person the interviewer likes and trusts, that's how. We'll talk more about how you can demonstrate these important qualities throughout the interview in the next chapter.

Exhibit your employability

Like people, different companies have different things they care about most – some care most about innovation, some about quality, some about value, some about social or environmental responsibility. They *all* care about the core workplace values we've been talking about though – intelligence, likeability, competence, integrity, positivity and adaptability. Employers care about these qualities in their employees because they all add up to a high degree of professionalism. And employers value professionalism because they can be tolerably certain that professionals will deliver high-quality work and do it to the best of their ability; take pride in their behaviour and appearance and represent the company advantageously; take every opportunity to learn and grow; and be enthusiastic about their work and positive about the organization and its aims and values.

In a recent survey by a US college, 90 per cent of the employers they contacted rated these sorts of workplace skills as 'important' or 'very important'. Compare this with the 25 per cent who put academic credentials alone in this top bracket. Similarly, a survey conducted by the UK Institute of Directors discovered that 88 per cent of employers considered these personal qualities to be as important or more important than academic ones.

Go back to the previous chapter and take another look at Exhibits 1 and 3. Think about how you can include evidence that demonstrates these highly employable qualities. How can you show that competence, integrity and adaptability, for example, are high on your list of workplace values? How can you use your industry knowledge to demonstrate your good cultural fit – that you care about the same things they care about?

Throughout the rest of this book, while we will concentrate on making sure all your relevant skills, competencies and experience are presented strongly and clearly, we will also be looking for every opportunity to demonstrate evidence of these other, more ephemeral personal attitudes and behaviours so that you can ensure that you come across as a highly employable candidate – one whom the company will be delighted to have on board and whose colleagues will be glad to work with them.

But first, there are steps you have to take to make sure that you remain the best possible *you* that you can be. Steps that will ensure that your qualities can shine through and show that you're the outstanding candidate that you really are.

You have to look after yourself.

Staying your best self

There's one skill that will make a huge difference to your search and to your life in general while you're job hunting.

You need resilience.

Job hunting is stressful. Waiting for replies is stressful. Worrying is stressful. Making calls is stressful. Preparing for interviews is stressful. Being in interviews is stressful. Being rejected is stressful. Picking yourself up and going for the next interview (and the next) is stressful.

Resilience is a skill that can be learnt like any other, and you need to look after yourself and practice some self-care. Taking time out to tend to yourself will not only keep you sane and healthy, it will actually make you more efficient. And when you do get that chance to shine, you'll be in exactly the right state to do so.

Take care of yourself

Feelings of frustration, doubt and anxiety are all perfectly normal during the job search. The interview you were banking on, doesn't come through; the one you had high hopes of ends in rejection. You have to keep going and move on to the next one with the same enthusiasm that you had at the beginning. It's hard, but you have to keep reminding yourself that feelings of hope, anticipation and achievement are all perfectly possible too.

To maintain a healthy balance – especially if you are between jobs – follow these self-care tips.

Give yourself a timetable

Being in work makes it easy to have a routine – you know when to get up, where to go and what to do every day. But if you're not in work, there's less pressure to get up, get dressed, or even go out at all. It's tempting to treat every day as a day off, but that's not helpful to you in the long run.

Make life easier by giving yourself a daily timetable to keep you on track and ensure you keep a sense of balance:

- Set your alarm for a reasonable time to get you out of bed.

- Decide how much time you'll spend job hunting each day, and when you're going to do it. Two or three hours of applied concentration should be enough – don't let it take over the whole of your life.

- You have time to prepare and eat proper meals – make the most of it. Good nutrition will boost your resilience enormously.

- Find time to socialize with others and try and make that actual contact when possible, not just social media browsing.

- Now could be the time to do all those things – the little jobs and chores – you've been meaning to get round to. Schedule them in but, again, don't let them take over.

- Get to bed and go to sleep at a regular time. Avoid the temptation of staying up binge-watching anything and everything. Now is a great opportunity to get eight hours sleep a night, every night, and help build up your resilience reserves.

Enjoy the up-sides

If you're not at work, there's no reason why your timetable can't benefit from the advantages of your situation.

You're free to go for walks, go to the park, enjoy your kids, travel outside the rush-hour, shop without battling the crowds – why not make the most of it? Build in a bit of flexibility to make the best use of your time.

Take breaks

For the two or three hours a day you're job hunting, give it your heart and soul. Then stop. It's easy to find yourself scrolling through job posting after job posting long after you've stopped taking anything in. Stop and do something else. Either move on to another job-hunting activity if it's still your job-hunting time, or go and do something completely different and come back to it fresh the next day.

Get outdoors

Make time every day to get out of doors and go for a walk. If you feel active, make it a run, bike-ride or workout, but get out into natural daylight for at least thirty minutes. Afterwards, you'll feel re-energized and less stressed, and the endorphins you generate will help keep your mood steady for the rest of the day. This could also be a good opportunity to improve your physical fitness and increase your physical resilience.

Set goals

As well as a timetable, you need to set goals for yourself. Clear daily, weekly and monthly goals will help keep you motivated and on course, especially when you feel you're losing sight of your aims–which can happen.

Break your job search down into a list of tasks such as writing your outline CV, getting a useful, adaptable covering letter ready, tweaking your LinkedIn page, etc, and allocate time to each one. Think of the things you have to do regularly such as making calls or posting CVs, and schedule them into your timetable – for example, network with ten people each week, two a day Monday to Friday.

Write your goals down rather than trying to keep it all in your head. It's much easier to keep on top of things if you just have to look at a list of objectives or your timetable when thinking what to do next, rather than trying to work out your tasks and priorities anew each and every time.

Your goals are targets to aim for. If you're reaching them easily – applying for two jobs a day, for instance–then increase your goal and stretch yourself a bit – aim to find three jobs a day to apply for, maybe. Don't set impossible goals from the start, tempting as it may be, and then feel a failure because you can't reach them. Setting goals that allow you to improve are much more encouraging and will keep you better motivated.

Avoid negativity

Now is the time to be kind to yourself and avoid self-criticism and negativity.

If you're looking for a job because you've just lost one, it's easy to question your self-worth. When employers don't get back to you or even reject you out-right, it's easy to let your insecurities get the better of you. It's only natural, but don't let it pull you into dwelling on negativity and self-criticism.

Be positive while allowing for the possibility of improvement. After each inter-view or any networking activity, review what went well, what you feel good about, and also what you could do differently next time. This way, you can look at your-self positively and recognize where your strengths lie, as well as looking at your-self objectively to see where small, continuous changes or improvements might add up to give you the edge.

For the most part, treat yourself like you would a good friend in the same situation – be as kind, positive, encouraging and understanding to yourself as you would be to them. Encouragement will motivate you to keep going; self-criticism will only demotivate you and make it more of an up-hill battle than it needs to be.

Celebrate all your successes

Don't wait until you reach the ultimate goal of a new job before you celebrate. Mark every success, however small, with some sort of recognition. The call you were so nervous about but went ahead and made anyway – celebrate it. The interview you fully prepared for – celebrate it. The positive feedback you received – celebrate it. Even if you've simply had an unusually purposeful, productive day – celebrate it.

It's easy to become focused on the big goals, but they can seem a dishearteningly long way off and you need to be aware of the progress you're making along the way. Keep your morale and motivation high by recognizing every triumph, public and private, and giving yourself a bit of applause and appreciation.

Share your wins with those close to you, and at the same time treat yourself to something you keep in reserve for just these occasions.

Remember who else you are

It's tempting to identify ourselves with the job that we do, maybe even over-identify a bit. If you're not currently at work all day, now could be the time to remember who else you are and what else you can do.

Set some personal goals as well as job search related ones. Find time to pursue neglected hobbies and skills, and maybe even try some new ones. If there's anything you ever wanted to learn, have a go at, or improve, this could be your chance. You have many more facets to your personality than can be accommodated in any job, and you have many more skills and attributes that you could be exploring and developing.

KEY TAKEAWAYS FROM CHAPTER 3

The interviewer is looking for more than just skills and qualifications, they're looking for employability.

- They don't just need to know that you can do the job, they need to be sure that you WILL do the job.
- They're looking for evidence of:

  contribution

cultural fit

motivation

engagement

- You will need to demonstrate that you have:

intelligence

likeability

competence

integrity

positivity

adaptability

- Improve your resilience and keep yourself in good shape to make sure that these qualities shine through.

4

ANSWERING QUESTIONS
WHAT THE INTERVIEWER WILL ASK AND WHAT YOU NEED TO TELL THEM

This is the main part of the book. From here on, you will find examples of the sort of questions asked at interview along with helpful ideas and suggestions for answering them.

Before we get on to what to say, however, let's look at how you say it. In this chapter we'll look at some general points about answering questions and how to put your answers across with confidence and enthusiasm.

Make a good impression

Overall impressions count for a lot at interview. Later, in Chapter 22, we'll look at creating a good first impression through how you dress, your body language and dealing with nerves. In this chapter, we look at creating the right impression through how you respond to questioning.

When you go into the interview, you have a full set of cards in your hand. They may be good cards, or not so good, but it's up to you to see you play them all and play them well. They are:

  your skills and abilities;

  your background and experience;

  your qualifications;

  your enthusiasm for a new opportunity;

  yourself – your personality and how you present yourself.

The interviewer already has an idea of your skills, qualifications and experience, and these are impressive enough for them to want to see you. What they don't have such a clear impression of are the last two items on the list: your personality and your enthusiasm. These are difficult to express on a CV or application form; you need to get them across at the interview because, as we saw in the previous chapter, it's precisely these personal qualities that can make you stand out as a highly employable candidate.

Don't put on an act and pretend to be some super-confident, super-bubbly or hard-nosed high-flyer if that's not the natural you. Be yourself, but be your best self. You know what you're like when you're happy, confident, vibrant and alert, and you know what you're like when you're crabby and stressed. They're both authentically you, but which one do you want to present at interview?

As we've seen, what organizations want from their workforce is contribution, cultural fit, motivation and engagement. There are some key personal qualities that help to guarantee this and are consequently always highly valued. It will help you a lot if you can express them at the interview. To recap, they are:

likeability;

intelligence;

positivity;

competence;

integrity;

adaptability.

To some extent these qualities overlap – competence often requires intelligence; positivity engenders likeability, and so on. However, we'll look at some general principals you can apply throughout the interview.

Likeability

You probably feel more comfortable with people who are friendly and open than with those who are reserved and stiff, and interviewers are no different.

Most employers want employees who are open, co-operative and communicative. They are much more pleasant to work with and get on with their colleagues better, so, naturally, they will be looking for these traits during the interview.

However nervous you feel, remember to smile. Be forthcoming; don't make the interviewer dig the information out of you. Avoid one-word, yes–no answers if you possibly can, and always give a full reply including relevant anecdotes as illustrations to key points. By being open and responsive, you will have a head start in presenting yourself well at interview.

Intelligence

Display your intelligence in a general way by being curious – asking questions and listening to the replies with interest. You can also subtly use questions to show your grasp of your profession and knowledge of the company. Asking questions will also demonstrate your enthusiasm for the sort of work you do and enthusiasm for the job you're applying for. Interviewers look more kindly on people who they feel will give 100 per cent than on those who may be better qualified on paper, but appear less wholehearted.

You don't have to gush; just be interested in what the interviewer is saying. Listen, smile and nod when they tell you things. When you answer, let your enthusiasm show in your anecdotes and illustrations, and in your questions to the interviewer (which we'll look at in Chapter 19). Genuine interest, sincerely shown, will increase your chances at interview enormously.

Positivity

Project energy and confidence – sit up straight, look alert, speak clearly, smile and make eye contact. When you appear energetic and lively, the interviewer sees someone positive, assured, optimistic and constructive – someone who will tackle problems rather than adding to them, and, crucially, someone who will be pleasant to work with.

Confident may be the last thing you feel when you go into the interview. Nevertheless, confidence is a key quality you must project. You needn't come across as pushy, smug or arrogant, but you do need to project a quiet, positive confidence in yourself and your abilities. The employer needs to be able to trust you to do the job. If you sound hesitant or uncertain, you undermine that trust.

Always answer positively too. People tend to take you at your own estimation, so don't put yourself down or apologize for what you see as shortcomings.

Example

The interviewer says, *'This job requires an understanding of spreadsheets. Would you say you had that?'*

You could put yourself down by replying: 'I'm sorry, I've used them to do the household accounts, but that's all, I'm afraid.'

Or you could give a positive impression by saying: 'Yes, I would. I use Microsoft Excel to do all the household accounts, so I'm quite used to it. I'm sure I could quickly become familiar with its commercial use.'

However nervous you are, make sure your voice sounds confident:

Pause and take a full breath before speaking. This relaxes your vocal cords and steadies your voice.

Speak a little lower than normal, projecting from your diaphragm rather than your throat. This stops your voice sounding shrill and strangled.

Speak a little slower and more clearly than you normally do. It stops you gabbling and saying things without thinking, and it gives you *gravitas*.

Remember to smile a few times during the interview; it warms up the voice and also helps you to relax your lip and cheek muscles.

You also need to be able to volunteer positive information about yourself and your abilities. In other words, you need to be able to blow your own trumpet. After all, they won't know how good you are unless you tell them. How do you put your points across without sounding as if you're bragging all the time? When you start to feel uncomfortable with 'I am...' and 'I can...', try ringing the changes with:

'I would say that I...';

'I believe I am...';

'My past record suggests...';

'My experience tells me...';

'People have told me I...';

'Colleagues tell me that...';

'My boss would probably say...';

'Friends say that I...'

Competence

The most basic way you can display competence is simply to turn up at the right place, on time and fully prepared. Present yourself well – well groomed and smart – and make sure you arrive with any material you may need such as a note-pad, a copy of your CV, any presentation materials you've been asked to bring, etc.

If you've been sent details of the interview in a contact letter or email keep it handy. Nerves could make you forget the name of the person who will be interviewing you, which floor of the building you need to get to, all sorts of things. It has been known for interviewees to turn up at large multi-occupancy office buildings only to find that, although they memorized the address, they've forgotten the name of the company actually holding the interview.

Integrity

Interviewers tend to rely on gut instinct to tell them whether or not someone is honest so demonstrate your trustworthiness in the traditional ways by offering a firm handshake, looking the interviewer in the eye, listening attentively and avoiding distracting nervous habits, They will, however, often ask questions that directly address this quality. Listen out for questions such as:

'What is the hardest professional hurdle you've ever had to face?'

'Can you describe a time at work when you had to ask for help from your manager?'

'Describe a time when you spoke out against general opinion.'

'In what areas are you weakest?'

'Describe a time when you had to admit to a mistake.'

'What is your attitude to risk?'

'Which sorts of clients do you find you have most problems with?'

'What sort of problems do you find hardest to deal with?'

Each of these questions – and others like them – is designed to evaluate the honesty, integrity and self-awareness of the candidate. We'll be looking at similar questions elsewhere in this book but, to generalize, you need to reflect on them and then answer honestly in a way relevant to the job in question. Don't be afraid of being honest – there is no one who doesn't have some weaknesses, or who finds all problems easy to handle. The interviewer will listen to your answer fairly, whatever it is, but any hint of bluff or bluster will be noted and could count against you far more negatively.

Adaptability

Throughout the interview, respond with positive energy and enthusiasm to the whole challenge of starting a new job and meeting new people. Demonstrate your adaptability by showing your willingness to learn and grow. Express an interest in developing your existing skills and knowledge further, and in opportunities for new experiences and responsibilities. And, of course, should anything unexpected happen during the interview, remain poised and react calmly and confidently. Show that you can adapt readily to the requirements of a changing situation.

Three cardinal rules

When answering the interviewer's questions, remember three cardinal rules:

Stick to the point.

Illustrate your answers with real-life anecdotes.

Don't waffle. When you've answered the question, stop talking.

Stick to the point

Listen to the question and make sure you answer it. Keep your answer relevant to the job you are interviewing for and don't go off at a tangent. Remember, most people have a two-minute attention span at the most, so practise keeping your answers shorter than this.

On the other hand, avoid simple yes–no answers unless the question clearly calls for no more than that.

If you're not sure you've understood the question, or you're not sure you've heard it properly, it's perfectly all right to ask the interviewer to repeat or rephrase it. It's much better to do that than to give an irrelevant answer.

Illustrate your answers with real-life anecdotes

Don't just say you can do x, y or z. Support your claim with concrete examples (see Chapter 2). Remember to stick to the point as outlined above – be concise and pick anecdotes that are appropriate for the job in question.

Don't waffle

When you've answered the question, stop talking. Don't let silence draw you into irrelevancies or, worse, negative revelations about yourself. When you've finished, add something like 'I hope that answers your question' or 'Does that cover all the points you need to know?' Then smile and wait for the next question.

One more cardinal rule: it always helps to imagine the words 'RELEVANT TO THIS JOB' after every question.

In the next chapter we'll look at the first few minutes of the interview – the welcome and the interviewer's opening questions. Knowing what to expect from the outset will help you to relax and put you at your ease so that you can concentrate on giving your best performance with confidence and style.

KEY TAKEAWAYS FROM CHAPTER 4

- If you lack confidence, you can benefit greatly from learning better interview skills.
- There are specific things you can learn to do that will help you to make a good impression every time.
- Even if you're already confident, you can still add things that will improve your performance.

WHAT THE EXPERT SAYS

I want to know how people react to things, what they do in certain situations. I want them to draw on their life experience. So when I ask what they would do in a crisis, for example, I don't want them to say 'I would do this; I would do that...' I want them to say 'I have done this; I have done that...'

Mark Colton, Business Development Team, Jobcentre Plus

WHAT THE EXPERT SAYS

People are hired for their skills. Don't let modesty prevent you from telling the interviewer about yourself, what you've done and the value of what you can do. Know yourself, what you're good at, and be comfortable and articulate talking about that.

David Giles, Resourcing Manager, Westland Helicopters Ltd

5

STARTING THE INTERVIEW
WHAT TO EXPECT FROM THE INTERVIEW AND HOW TO BEGIN CONFIDENTLY

This is it: you're in the interview, sitting opposite the interviewer. What happens now?

We'll talk about how you got there – entering the room, shaking hands with the interviewer and lots of other details about making a good first impression – in Chapter 21, Looking the part. But for now, let's look at how the interviewer will start the interview and their opening questions to you.

Your interviewer will probably open the interview with a brief introductory chat about the company, the job, the form the interview will take, etc. There will also be general 'social' questions designed to break the ice:

'Did you have a good journey?'

'Was the traffic OK?'

'Did you find the building/your way here all right?'

Beware. The impression you give in these first few minutes will linger throughout the rest of the interview. Although the questions are genuinely meant to put you at your ease, your responses will still form a picture of you in the interviewer's mind.

Remember you are here to demonstrate, along with your skills and experience, your:

likeability;

intelligence;

positivity;

competence;

integrity;

adaptability.

So don't:

Gabble feverishly. You should have enough competence to get there in time to regain both your breath and composure. If nerves are a problem, see Chapter 21 for tips on dealing with them.

Clam up. Be co-operative and friendly, and try to give more than a terse, one-word answer.

Complain. Be positive. However bad the traffic, however difficult the office was to find, don't make an issue of it: 1) you'll be seen as a moaner; 2) they'll wonder how you cope with other minor problems and irritations; 3) you'll be making the same journey every day if they employ you, so are they going to have to listen to you complain every time?

Blame. Don't pick faults in their directions or instructions even if you could improve on them.

Ramble. Be professional. This is not the time for lengthy answers about routes, timetables, maps, etc.

Put yourself down. You don't need to explain how disorganized you are or what a poor sense of direction you have.

Use problems as an excuse. Cope with adversity. They won't see being stuck in a traffic jam that morning as a reason for doing badly in the interview.

Do demonstrate your likeability, competence and positivity from the start:

Smile. Do your share of the ice breaking by smiling and making eye contact.

Answer warmly and pleasantly. Behave as you would in any somewhat formal social situation.

Give a positive response. Whatever the circumstances, give the impression of being calm and in control.

See Chapter 22 for more tips on creating a good first impression.

After putting you at your ease, the interviewer will sometimes lead into the main part of the interview by asking you an open question such as *'Tell me about yourself'* or *'Tell me about your current job.'* They want to know about your competencies, so this is your invitation to sell your ability and experience. Think of it as a mini-interview in which you briefly introduce topics that the interviewer can explore in greater depth with their subsequent questions.

Q 'Tell me about yourself.'

This is as open as a question can be. Remember that from the very outset of the interview, your aim is to demonstrate your suitability for the job. Consequently, it's up to you to set the boundaries and make sure you stick to points that are informative and relevant. The interviewer wants you to include things like:

your current position;

your background, education and training;

the skills and strengths that make you good at your job;

your experience and accomplishments;

the high points of your career so far;

the contribution you have made in your current role;

what attracted you to your particular field and how you got into it;

your goals for the future.

You need, of course, to tailor your answer and take into consideration the skills, strengths, aptitudes and experience – the competencies – required for the job along with your personal qualities.

Example

'I'm a [give a concise, pithy description of yourself in 15 words or less]. I'm an experienced [whatever you are] with an extensive knowledge of [your relevant knowledge area] including [a key point] and [another key point]. My main skills or qualifications are [give two or three of your most relevant skills or your key qualifications].

'I also have experience in [go on to your next most relevant skill or knowledge area], including [develop one or two key points].

'My achievements to date include [two or three of your major achievements]. The benefits to my current employer have been [outline the benefits – whatever you've increased, decreased or improved] and I believe that I have [contributed x] to [the team, project, department or company]. I believe the position you're offering would allow me to [what you want to go on to do or develop].'

Example

'I'm a computer science graduate with a keen interest in the practical application of information systems. I'm an experienced computer programmer with an extensive knowledge of robotics including 3-D modelling and components assembly. My main skills are programming methodologies and microelectronics.

'I also have experience in artificial intelligence, including Popll and Prologue.

'My main achievement to date has been to write a geographical database using a GIS package, which allowed NHS patient data to be mapped for the entire West Midlands region. This greatly improved allocation of resources to high-density areas, and reduced patient waiting time by 11 per cent overall, and I believe that my ability to work well with the development team and to liaise with NHS representatives throughout the process contributed to the project's efficiency and success. I believe the position you're offering would allow me to continue to develop my problem-solving skills and I feel I could contribute skills and experience that would be of value to you.'

Note that this answer not only gives a full account of the interviewee's considerable skills and experience, it also demonstrates their interpersonal skills, including their ability to work comfortably as part of a team, communicate complex information to others involved with the project and take responsibility for keeping other concerned participants informed.

Q 'Give me an outline of your current position.'

This question focuses more closely on your actual job. It is practically asking for your current job description to see how well it matches the job you're applying for. The interviewer wants to know things like:

- what your tasks and responsibilities are;
- the skills required to do your job;
- the strengths and personal aptitudes you bring to it;
- the key objectives of your job;
- targets and result criteria;
- whom you answer to – your position in the company hierarchy and level of authority.

Base your answer on the example above, incorporating all the relevant information.

Q 'What does your current job entail? Describe a typical day to me.'

With this question, the interviewer is looking for a more personal interpretation of your job. They want to see how you view your tasks and responsibilities. They want to know:

what you see as the prime purpose of your job;

the tasks and responsibilities your job entails;

the skills, strengths and aptitudes you employ;

the problems you routinely encounter and how you deal with them effectively;

how you work with others – as part of a team, dealing with staff, meeting customers or clients, etc;

what you enjoy and find satisfying about your job.

After hearing your answers to these sorts of open questions, the interviewer will usually go on to ask other questions to fill in more details – *'Tell me more about x,' 'Can you say a bit more about y?'*

Answer in more detail, bearing in mind the relevance of your points to the job you are interviewing for, and supply anecdotes to illustrate and support what you are saying.

Example

Q 'Can you tell me more about how you get the best out of your team?'

'I believe that people work best when they're given responsibility. For example, we had a problem meeting sales targets in the Colchester area. Rather than just harassing the team to get better results, I put it to them as a group problem and asked them to come up with a workable solution. After a couple of brainstorming sessions, they came up with a member-get-a-member scheme based on the upcoming festival. They were responsible for implementing it while I saw they had the back-up needed from Head Office. Sales increased by 40 per cent over the festival, and subsequently steadied to 22 per cent, well within target.'

Note how this answer demonstrates mature team-working skills including intelligence, competence, adaptability and positivity.

Example

Q 'Can you tell me more about how you fit into the organization? You work alone currently, don't you?'

'I'm at the selling end of the operation, representing the company to the public. But, even though I work alone, I still see myself as part of a wider team with the same goals and values. I have strong links to Head Office and really appreciate the help and support they give. I'm also ready to support them in any way I can. For example, when stocktaking was done recently, Head Office decided it would be quicker and more efficient if it was done in teams of three rather than each of us doing just our own. I thought this was a good idea and was happy to travel to another branch in return for help with my own stocktake. It made what could have been a rather long and tedious job much quicker and more enjoyable.'

Note how this answer demonstrates shared values along with agreeableness, positivity and adaptability.

These more probing questions lead naturally into the main part of the interview. We'll discuss this in detail in Chapter 8 onwards, with examples of questions asked at interviews for different types of jobs along with suggestions for the best ways of answering them – from the straightforward ones to the decidedly tricky.

First, though, let's look at the questions they ask everybody – those general questions that seem to crop up at interview after interview – and how you can use them to your advantage.

KEY TAKE-AWAYS FROM CHAPTER 5

- Knowing what to expect at the interview will increase your confidence.
- You can't help making a first impression, so make sure it's a good one.
- Listen. The opening questions may offer you a great opportunity to present your key skills and qualities right from the beginning.

WHAT THE EXPERT SAYS

Listen to the question before you try to answer it. You've got two ears and one mouth; they're in that ratio for a reason.

Janet Hembry, Head of Education and Skills Policy,
Government Office for the South West

6

QUESTIONS THEY ASK EVERYBODY

STANDARD QUESTIONS YOU SHOULD PREPARE FOR

In the rest of this book we'll be looking in detail at the questions asked during interviews for different types of jobs and the best ways of answering them. In many cases, even when the questions are the same, the answers – and what the interviewer is hoping to find out – will have a different emphasis, so it's worth having different sections that focus exclusively on the requirements of each particular sort of job.

There are some questions, however, that are pretty much the same for everyone, whatever the job is. Look at the ones here and consider how you would reply. The answers given here and throughout *Ultimate Interview* are intended to get you thinking about your own particular circumstances. You don't have to learn them parrot-fashion; adapt them to your own style of speaking so that you can say what *you* want to say. They do, though, cover the main points that you will need to think about. They can help you plan your responses ahead of the interview so that you are rarely, if ever, caught unprepared.

It's unlikely you'll be asked all these questions, or that they'll be phrased in precisely these words, but being prepared means you'll be able to answer any similar questions confidently.

Q 'Why do you want to work here?'

This is a great opportunity to demonstrate your cultural fit with the company as well as your motivation and enthusiasm for making a contribution. If you've done the preparation suggested in Chapter 2, you should have a clear idea of how this job fits into your career plan and why the company is the right one for you. Good reasons to concentrate on are those things that allow you to work at your best. These include the company structure, reputation, conditions, management methods, opportunity, challenge, etc. Follow up with the positive things you will be able to contribute to the company under those conditions.

Example

'I believe [company name] is a progressive company providing a challenging, stimulating and supportive environment for its employees and their achievements [or whatever else you value – the opportunity for rapid advancement, creative freedom or technical innovation]. I have x years' experience in [your field of work] and my time at [the company you work for] has shown me I have a talent for [a skill or ability highly relevant to the job you're applying for]. I think I've demonstrated that by [mention an achievement and what you're contributed]. I am now looking for the opportunity to continue to achieve at that level and beyond, in a company that will help me develop professionally. I believe your company offers just such an opportunity.'

Example

'I take pride in my work and like to be fully involved with the whole process rather than just my little bit of it [for example]. I believe the team-based structure employed by [the interviewing company] and your use of performance bonuses [for example] encourage a greater involvement and demand more of a sense of responsibility both individually and as a team member.'

Example

'I'm looking for a position where I can use my [a relevant skill, aptitude or area of experience] to make a strong contribution to [the profession, the company the team, whatever is most appropriate]. I believe this job would allow me to make the most of my [a talent, aptitude, skill or ability] along with [another skill, personal quality or ability]. I see it, above all, as a natural development from [your experience, further qualifications or training].'

Q 'What interests you most about this job?'

This is an opportunity to demonstrate your motivation, engagement and contribution. Concentrate on what you will bring to the job rather than what you believe you can get out of it. The interviewer needs to know you are enthusiastic about using your skills, abilities and experience to benefit the company. In answering the question, remind them of the skills that mean you *can* do the job and the personal qualities that mean you *will* do the job. Add your reasons for wanting to change jobs, and your reasons for wanting to work for the company if those questions haven't already been dealt with.

Example

'I'm looking for a position where I can use my [one or two of your key abilities] to the full. I believe this job would allow me to make the most of those along with my [another skill or personal quality]. I see it as a natural development from [your experience and achievements]. I've enjoyed working in [your current job], especially [mention a key feature], but they're a small company and unfortunately there's no opportunity for advancement with them in the near future [for example]. I believe an expanding company [for example] such as yours offers a greater range of challenges and opportunities, in particular [a key responsibility or competency mentioned in the job description that you would like to develop further].'

Q 'What experience do you have for this job?'

The interviewer wants to know you fully understand what the job requires. They also want to be sure you're capable of taking over the job smoothly without a long, disruptive adjustment period. If you've done your homework, you'll have already matched your skills, strengths and experience to those required in the job description, and be ready to point out how good a match you are.

Example

'I have x years' experience working in [your relevant background]. My achievements include [give examples]. My background in [the relevant experience you've had or positions you've held] and familiarity with [a process, piece of equipment, working environment, for example] would allow me to contribute to the job from the start. I understand [one or two key things from the job description that demonstrate you know what the job involves], and the importance of [a personal quality from the job description]. These have been essential elements in my current job and I appreciate their importance. In addition, I have an excellent record of [a key ability you've found essential to carry out your work effectively]. For example, [give a short anecdote demonstrating this skill or quality, and its benefits].'

Q 'How has your job changed since you've been there?'

The interviewer really wants to know if your responsibilities have increased. Demonstrate your engagement and motivation and tell them about any extra tasks or responsibilities you've taken on, and any skills and qualities you've developed or training you've undertaken. You can also demonstrate your adaptability. They also want to know how you respond to change – do you react well or do you resent it? It's unusual for any job to stay the same, so tell them what changes have happened in your job, including different working methods, different tasks, different management, etc. Emphasize that you adapted to the changes easily and found them beneficial. Give the impression that you are positive and flexible.

Q 'Do you have more responsibilities now than when you started?'
Q 'Have your responsibilities increased while you've been doing your current job?'

Tell the interviewer about any extra tasks or responsibilities you've taken on and, especially, any promotions you've received. Even if your duties haven't increased officially, it's almost certain that you've taken on more responsibilities as you've got to know the job and become more confident.

Example

'Yes, my responsibilities have increased substantially. When I first started, my supervisor [manager, boss] had to instruct me about every job and check my work at each stage. I made mistakes in the beginning, naturally, but it meant I learnt how to [do what you do] thoroughly, and I learnt how to work efficiently and to a high standard. With time, I became more confident about what I was doing and took responsibility for [list some of your tasks], and eventually [name something you became responsible for]. These days, my supervisor just gives me the work schedule [or whatever] and I plan the work order and carry it out [for example]. I believe the confidence my supervisor now has in my ability shows how I've developed in the job, and that I'm now ready to take on greater responsibilities.'

Note how this answer neatly demonstrates adaptability, positivity, integrity, competence and intelligence.

Q 'What has your current job taught you?'
Q 'What did you learn from your last job?'

Most companies like a level of maturity and flexibility in their staff. They like to know that you are capable of learning from experience and can accept constructive advice. Reflect this in your answer and choose a key point from each of the following:

a personal quality you've developed or realized the value of;

a responsibility you've taken on;

a practical skill you've developed.

Pick a brief anecdote that shows you using them. Remember, too, that what you've learnt must be relevant to the job you're applying for, not just the one you've been doing.

Example

'I'm always happy to learn on the job and I believe my last position taught me a number of things. I learnt how to [include a skill] and I developed [another skill or ability] further. I also developed [a responsibility or role you took on]. I would say that in that job I also learnt the importance of [a personal quality or workplace skill you learnt the value of]. For example, [give a brief anecdote].'

Q 'Do you prefer working alone or with others?'

You will know from the job description whether the job involves primarily working alone or in a team, so tailor your answer accordingly. However, whatever job you do, you have to get on with others and there will be times, even as a team member, when you have to work on your own. Reassure the interviewer you'd be happy in either role and demonstrate your innate agreeableness and adaptability.

Example

'I've worked as a team member in [give a specific situation], and I've worked on my own in [give another situation]. I'm happy to do either depending on the requirements of the job. I've found, though, that working in [whichever the job requires] allows me to [give some positive benefit of either working with others or alone].'

Q 'How well do you work in a team?'

Presumably, you'll be working in a team if you get the job or they wouldn't ask. Therefore, your answer is that you work very well in a team. Anyone can claim that, though, so illustrate your answer with an anecdote about a time you successfully worked in a team and enjoyed it. If you can't give an example from the workplace, use a sport or other activity to illustrate your answer.

Example

'I would say from past experience that I enjoy being part of a team. I like the camaraderie and that feeling of all working together towards a common goal [for example]. I believe a good team member should be [see the list in the next question for a selection of positive qualities] and I try to demonstrate these qualities when working with others. For example, in my last job, [give your example of working well in a team, demonstrating at least one key quality from the list].'

Q 'What makes a good team member?'

Good team members are:

communicative;

supportive of the other members;

flexible – they can fit in with others and adapt to changing demands;

unselfish – they put the needs of the other team members on a level with their own;

interested in the success of the team as a whole, and making a positive contribution to that, not just their own performance.

As above, illustrate your answer with times when you've displayed these qualities.

Q 'Why do you want to change jobs?'
Q 'What were your reasons for leaving your last job?'

You must have a positive answer ready. If the interviewer asks you this question, they are trying to find out if there's anything that should sound alarm bells for them:

Are you changing jobs because you've been sacked?

Are you leaving because of a personality clash with your boss or a colleague?

Have you been passed over for promotion or some similar reason?

Negative reasons such as that you didn't get on with your boss, or were asked to leave for any reason except job redundancy, will go down badly. Even just being vague might make the interviewer wonder if you are prone to changing jobs on a whim.

Good reasons for changing jobs are:

Challenge. You want more demanding tasks and responsibilities which demonstrates your motivation and eagerness to contribute.

Reputation. As long as you don't cast a slur on your present employer, applying to a more prestigious company is an acceptable reason for wanting to change jobs especially when you can demonstrate a better cultural fit. If you're proud of your skills, why not use them for the best in the business?

Promotion. If the job you're applying for is a step up from your current one, naturally you'd go for it, especially if the structure of your present company doesn't allow you to develop further.

Opportunity. You want the chance to work on something different or develop in a particular way with more opportunity for engagement and the chance of making a bigger contribution.

Security. This can be a convincing reason for some jobs. There's no harm in wanting a more secure job with a more stable company especially when you can highlight your own steadiness and dependability along with your steadfast values.

Location. If the company you're applying to is in a better or more convenient place, you could mention this as a contributing factor, but try not to make it your main reason.

Money. Your salary may no longer reflect your experience or value to the company. Again, though, try not to give this as your main or only reason.

Start by saying that you enjoy your current job and give brief details of what you enjoy and why. Go on to explain why, despite that, you want to change, using the reasons above as a guide.

Example

'I've enjoyed working [where you work or what you do], especially the opportunity they've given me to [mention something you've achieved and/or contributed]. They're a small company, though, [for example] and unfortunately there's no opportunity for advancement with them in the near future [the promotion reason].'

Example

'I enjoy my job as a [what you do], and I've enjoyed working at [where you work]. I've particularly appreciated [mention a few key points about your role or the working conditions you've benefited from]. However, I've developed my bookkeeping skills [for example] over the past year or so, and I now find this side of the job more appealing. Unfortunately, a suitable position using these skills is unlikely to arise in the near future so I'm looking for a post where I can develop them more fully [the opportunity reason]. I believe this job offers just such an opportunity.'

Before we go on to look at specific questions for specific types of job, we need to look in more detail at a certain type of question the interviewer might ask you.

While the general advice of this book is always to answer any questions except the most basic, straightforward ones with anecdotes that illustrate your past experience and the skills that make you suitable for the job, there is a specific sort of question that absolutely *demands* that you provide a full description of how you have dealt with past situations and events at work. These are called 'behavioural questions' and they are designed to show the interviewer how you have performed in the past and therefore how you are likely to perform in the future.

KEY TAKE-AWAYS FROM CHAPTER 6

- There are some questions that are more or less standard for every job.
- You can do your research and prepare thorough answers to these questions well before the interview.
- Preparing beforehand gives you time to consider and rehearse how you'll include all your key skills and qualities when the relevant questions arise.

WHAT THE EXPERT SAYS

My advice to anyone would be: think; don't rush. Stop and take in the question. Make sure you understand what the interviewer wants to know and think about the answer. Make sure you answer the whole question.

Maggie Fellows, Project Manager, TUC

7

BEHAVIOURAL QUESTIONS
SOME QUESTIONS DIG DEEPER THAN OTHERS

The chapters that follow focus on questions for specific types of job. Different jobs demand a different set of abilities, and the interviewer's questions take this into account.

Before we look at the details, though, we need to look at some questions that are designed to dig deeply into not just what you can do, but how you actually do it.

Interviewing is becoming more of a science that an art. In an increasing number of interviews, you'll find the interviewer will have a list of the six or seven key competencies – skills, abilities and experience – specified for the job, and will ask you six or seven questions about times when you've demonstrated exactly those competencies. These are known as 'behavioural questions', and you'll recognize them because they are the questions that start 'Can you give me an example of when you've done X' or 'Tell me about a time when you demonstrated Y'. Although they may ask further questions to clarify points or draw out more details from you, those six or seven questions are the core of the interview.

The aim of these questions is not just to assess your past experience, but to go beyond your technical competencies and to try and discover the personal qualities you bring into play during your working life. Your answer will reveal not just your skills and abilities, but your approach to work and your personality.

It is essential that you:

- read the job description and the job posting thoroughly;

- list the competencies asked for in them;

- have ready real-life examples and anecdotes of times when you've used them.

Respond to this types of question with a specific example of how you have dealt with the situation in the past, giving a brief (but comprehensive) anecdote that covers all the important points.

What are the important points?

A very useful technique for making sure you've covered all the key points is call the STAR strategy. This gives you a four-step method to help you organize your thoughts and deliver a comprehensive answer. STAR stands for:

Situation – explain the situation where the event took place.

Task – describe the task you were faced with, including any special problems or considerations you had to bear in mind.

Action – give details about the actions you took to resolve the situation. Don't forget to cover all the key skills you used.

Result – don't forget to say what the result of your action was, focusing on the benefits to the company, your clients and colleagues.

Take your time to answer the question – the interviewer won't mind if you take a moment to reflect on what they are asking. With good preparation – and a bit of luck – you should already have a clear idea of which skills and competencies are likely to be under scrutiny and so have an example which fits the bill. Use the STAR technique to help you structure your answer – starting at the beginning with the situation in which it took place, and ending with the beneficial results of your action. Be positive even if you are being asked to focus on a problem or a failure. Describe the issues fully but briefly then turn your main focus onto the solution of the problem and the positive result.

There are examples of behavioural questions throughout the following chapters, but here are two that break down the answer into its component parts.

Example:

Q: Have you ever made a mistake in your job? What did you do to correct it?

Situation: We used to run projects on yearly cycles at XYZ except one came up that the client needed in nine months. I was project manager and planned accordingly. However, I hadn't taken into consideration that there would be a ten-day shut-down over the holiday period.

> **Task:** I had to re-schedule the project within an already tight time-frame, keeping the team on board with the changes and make sure we delivered a first-rate result for a very important client.
>
> **Action:** I decided the key was ensuring everything was ready before the shut-down so we could pick it up again with the minimum delay. I scheduled actions, briefed suppliers, and organized team members with this in mind.
>
> **Result:** When the shutdown came, everything was right on track. The team came back from the break relaxed, unpressurized and eager to get on with the project. We even had time to add a couple of refinements. The client was delighted and placed several subsequent orders.

Example:

Q: Tell me about a time you had to handle a difficult staffing problem.

> **Situation:** When I was department supervisor at ABC, one of the staff who had always been very reliable became much less so. It wasn't only her performance that was the problem; the other staff were complaining about covering for her mistakes.
>
> **Task:** I had to find out what the problem was and get everyone back on track again before our department targets were affected.
>
> **Action:** I had an informal chat with her over coffee during the break and found out she had major problems at home that she was trying to sort out during worktime, taking time and attention off her job. We discussed some options and finally agreed that it would be better if she actually took a couple of days off to address the problem. She could give it her full attention and I could get someone to officially cover for her.
>
> **Result:** This meant that everybody knew what they were doing – her responsibilities were covered, the complaints stopped and she came back after a couple of days fully focused on her work. I had a happy, productive team again and the department met its quarterly target.

There could well be further interview questions that follow on from these answers. For example, a follow-on question from the first answer might be: 'How exactly did you ensure that the team was kept on board with these changes?' Another could be: 'How did you ensure that suppliers delivered on time?'

You can see how questions like this begin to build up a picture for the interviewer of how you have performed in the past and how you are likely to perform in the future.

However the interviewer sets about interviewing you and whatever the type of question they ask you, your key task always is to demonstrate your suitability for the job and to demonstrate those highly employable personal qualities that will make you stand out.

The next eight chapters focus on specific questions for specific types of job. Again, whatever the job, *your key task always is to demonstrate your suitability for the job and to demonstrate those highly employable personal qualities that will make you stand out.*

Find the chapter that relates most closely to the sort of work you're interviewing for – clerical, technical, practical, creative etc. Read the questions and prepare your answers. Although they may not be worded in exactly the same way, the questions are typical of the sort asked. Even if you aren't asked these exact questions, preparing the answers will take you through key points so you'll be well equipped to answer confidently, whatever form the questions take. You may not use all the answers you've prepared, but having gone through them and knowing the information is there at your fingertips will give you the sort of confidence that shines through at interview.

Prepare your answers then practise, practise, practise delivering them so that you can do it even in the stress of an interview. Friends or family can help – even better if they can reword the questions so that you don't know exactly what's coming and have to think about your response. It will help you to be flexible and able to think on your feet without losing your nerve.

KEY TAKE-AWAYS FROM CHAPTER 7

The interviewer isn't just interested in what you can do, but in how you have done it in the past.

Don't let behavioural questions catch you by surprise – you can prepare for them beforehand:

- Understand the key competencies required to do the job.
- Think about a range of specific situations in which you've used these skills and qualities.
- Make sure you cover the main points by using the STAR method.
- Take your time, listen to the question and think about your answer.
- Preparing your answers in this way is never a waste of time - you can always use the information to give full and detailed answers to any type of question you get asked.

WHAT THE EXPERT SAYS

We need people with a very broad set of skills. The perfect way to find the ideal employee would be to get them in and have them do the job. We can't do that at the moment, although that day may come, so the next best thing is to ask them what they have done in the past in similar circumstances to the ones they will meet here. That way we can see if they have the experience we need and whether their priorities and actions show them as the sort of person who will work well in a place like this.

Senior manager, project agency

8

QUESTIONS FOR PRACTICAL JOBS
CORE QUESTION: 'ARE YOU RELIABLE?'

Typical jobs:

maintenance worker;

warehouse worker;

catering worker;

assembly worker;

driver;

carer;

appliance repairer;

construction worker;

service engineer;

mechanic;

fitter;

dental assistant;

grounds keeper;

furniture maker;

animal handler;

health and safety;

heating engineer;

horticulturist;

hospital porter;

machinist.

Businesses need reliable people to do the practical jobs such as building maintenance, deliveries, security and line work.

They need to know that the nuts-and-bolts hands-on jobs will be done dependably. If they aren't, other employees won't be able to do their own work. If there's no one to carry out these key roles accurately, effectively and efficiently, the whole organization quickly falls apart. Consequently, dependable, trustworthy people are absolutely vital for practical jobs.

The key thing the interviewer will be trying to find out is: *'Are you reliable?'* They need to know if you'll be able to do the job competently and dependably. In other words, are you a safe pair of hands? Keep in mind the key qualities needed for most practical jobs. These are:

knowledge and hands-on experience of the job;

competence and reliability;

self-reliance as well as the ability to follow instructions accurately;

flexibility and adaptability;

recognized training such as BTEC, HNC or HND.

The interviewer wants you to demonstrate clearly that you know *what* needs to be done and that you know *how* to do it. One of the most important things to emphasize, therefore, is your experience. When you're going through the questions and preparing your answers, focus your attention on:

The sort of experience you have. Look at the work you have done in the past and in your current position. Focus particularly on the tasks and responsibilities. Look at the experience you have gained in each job, the specific responsibilities you have had, and the skills you have developed through doing it.

Your key skills. Concentrate on the practical skills that you need for your job and that have proved useful in the past. Make it clear that you understand what the job requires and that you know how to deliver it. If you have training, or if you have specific qualifications – an HGV licence, for example, or a Hygiene Certificate – don't forget to mention them in your answers.

Your personal qualities. You know which qualities have proved useful in your job – things such as patience or confidence in dealing with the public, for example. Mention them and how useful they have been to you in your work. Provide anecdotes about when and where you've used them. You'll also need anecdotes that clearly show your:

- competence and dependability;
- self-reliance;
- flexibility;
- ability to follow instructions accurately and find out further information where necessary.

Keep these important points in mind when thinking about your answers to the questions that follow.

Q 'What are your greatest strengths?'
Q 'What are your best qualities?'

When you're looking for a practical job, focus on your practical qualities. Ideally, one of your greatest strengths will be your experience, and another your reliability. Give some solid examples of how, where and when you've demonstrated these qualities. Stick to three or four key points and put them across strongly.

Example

'I would say my greatest strengths with regard to this job are my experience, my reliability, my [a skill] and my [a personal quality]. I have x years' experience working in [your relevant background] and my knowledge of [tasks you've done or responsibilities you've held] and familiarity with [a relevant process or piece of equipment] mean that I would be able to do the work competently and efficiently. I believe my current/previous employer would agree that I can be relied on to do the job even under difficulties/pressure. For example, [describe a time you did that].'

Example

'I believe that my [your most relevant skill] would be valuable in this job. It would allow me to [explain why this skill is important]. Another strength I can bring to the job is my [your key personal quality]. I've found it to be of great importance in my current/previous job as it means that [explain why this quality has been helpful to you in the past].'

Q 'Why should I hire you?'

The interviewer might throw this question in as a challenge. React calmly and consider your answer.

Example

'I think you should hire me because I believe I have the skill and experience to do the job reliably and dependably.' (If you haven't already covered them, now is a good time to outline your key strengths. See the previous question for more details about doing that.)

Q 'What are your qualifications for this job?'

Give any qualifications you have, along with any training. Don't forget vocational qualifications and on-the-job training as well, as this can often be more useful than classroom-based training. Follow up with a brief rundown of your experience as this is often more important in practical jobs than paper qualifications.

Example

'I have [your qualifications – BTEC, HNC, HND, etc]. I've also been trained in [any relevant on-the-job training]. I believe, though, that my best qualification for the job is my x years' experience. I have [give your relevant employment history]. My practical knowledge of [the tasks you've done or responsibilities you've held] and familiarity with [a relevant process or piece of equipment], along with my training, mean I would be able to do the work competently and efficiently.'

Q 'What would you say makes a good... [what your job is]?'
Q 'What makes you a good... [what your job is]?'

You've read the job description, so you know what *they* think makes a good whatever your job is. Match this to your own skills, strengths and personal qualities. Emphasize your practical abilities and reliability.

Q 'How well do you work without supervision?'

If they ask you this question, it's likely the job involves working without supervision for large parts of the time. Your answer must therefore be positive. They want to know if you will:

get on with the job even when no one's looking over your shoulder;

take responsibility for your work;

make appropriate decisions;

take action in everyday situations;

solve everyday problems.

It's rare for someone to have never worked unsupervised and have no experience to draw on. However, even if you have little experience, there are sure to have been times in your personal life when you've successfully completed tasks or projects on your own that you can refer to.

Examples

'In my previous job as a [what you did], I often worked alone without direct supervision for long periods of time because [explain why – you worked off-site, you had no direct line manager]. I would consult [whoever you consulted] when there was a technical problem [or other problem outside your responsibility], but otherwise I planned my own work and handled everyday problems and decisions myself.'

'In my previous job as a [give your work experience], I worked without direct supervision for short periods of time when [explain the circumstances]. However, I'm an experienced DIYer [for example] and have carried out many home projects without supervision, so I'm used to planning my own work and handling practical problems and decisions myself. For example, I have to [outline how you plan and organize your work].'

Q 'What qualities do you need to work unsupervised?'

As above, the underlying question is *'Can you work without supervision?'* The skills you need to work unsupervised are:

self-discipline – the ability to tackle tasks and meet deadlines and targets without being chased up all the time;

self-motivation – the ability to carry out your responsibilities without constant encouragement;

self-reliance – the ability to resolve everyday problems and make straightforward decisions on your own.

Mention these skills and go on to say when and where you've demonstrated them.

Q 'What kinds of decisions do you make independently in your current job?'

This is a straightforward question about your responsibilities, but it still helps to have thought about it before the interview. Most people underestimate what they do until they actually go through it all.

> **Example**
>
> 'In my job as a [what you do] I'm responsible for everything to do with [what you're responsible for]. I consult [whoever you consult] when there's a technical problem [or other problem outside your responsibility], but otherwise I plan my own work and handle everyday problems and decisions myself. For example, [give examples of the sort of decisions you take in a normal day and how you deal with them].'

Q 'Have you ever had any problems with supervisors?'

Obviously, the answer is 'No'.

> **Example**
>
> 'No, I've never had any problems that I can think of. Supervisors are there to see that the job gets done and I understand that it sometimes entails guidance and constructive criticism.'

Q 'Would you say you follow instructions well?'

Even though the question invites it, avoid saying just 'Yes' or 'No'. Illustrate your answer with an anecdote or example.

> **Example**
>
> 'Yes, I would say I take instructions well. Like most people, I prefer it when I'm given reasons and explanations for things, and my current supervisor is usually very good about that, although I realize it's not always possible under pressure. I make sure I've clarified the information before I carry out the task, and I feed back the results to my supervisor afterwards if necessary. For example, [give an example of a time you did that].'

Q 'What have you done that shows initiative?'

Ideally, as well as following instructions, you should be able to think for yourself and act on your own initiative when the need arises. Think of a time when you acted responsibly and resolved a problem or made a decision. Choose an occasion when you acted responsibly and avoid anything that makes you look rash or impulsive.

Q 'How do you decide when it's appropriate to use your initiative or better to refer to your manager?'

In other words, how do you balance following instructions with thinking for yourself? You need to give a balanced answer in response.

Example

'On the whole, the company I currently work for sets out clear guidelines about what decisions I can make and what options are practical [you are used to making everyday decisions]. They also have clear procedures for most circumstances and I would generally follow those [you can understand and follow instructions]. However, if a situation arose where there were no guidelines, it was urgent or I was unable to contact my supervisor, I would do my best to make a decision based on the facts, using my experience of similar circumstances. I would keep a record of my actions and inform my manager as soon as possible. For example, [tell them about a time when you did that].'

Q 'Do you get bored doing routine work?'

The job has a high proportion of routine work or they wouldn't be asking you, so the answer is 'No'. Avoid the simple one-word answer, though.

Example

'No, I don't really get bored. I have a methodical approach to things and enjoy doing a thorough job.'

Q 'Are you reliable?'

Yes, of course you are – one of the key things they're looking for is reliability. Illustrate your reply with an anecdote demonstrating your dependability.

Example

'I believe that I am and I think my present company would agree that I am, too. I have an excellent timekeeping and attendance record, and I take my responsibilities seriously, completing [what it is you have to do] on time and to a high standard. I have to be reliable in my work as a [what you do], because if I don't do my job other people can't do theirs. So it's important to me that I do a good job even when it takes extra effort. For example, [give an example of when you had to overcome a problem or setback and make an extra effort to get a job done, and the resulting benefit to the company].'

Q 'Do you think speed or accuracy is the more important?'

They want both, so you need to convince them that you are both fast *and* accurate.

Example

'I believe both are important. I try to manage my workload so that both are achievable. Fortunately, my experience means that I am able to work to a high speed while maintaining quality.'

Q 'What are some of the problems you encounter in your job?'
Q 'Tell me about a problem you've had to deal with.'

All jobs involve a degree of problem solving, but they don't just want to know what the problems are; they want to know how you resolve them. Stick to practical problems and avoid anything that suggests a problem getting on with people, difficulties with management, or anything that could be seen as a criticism of your current employer. When you tell them how you dealt with the issue, include the following points:

You stayed calm.

You were clear-headed.

Experience and common sense helped you find the solution.

You kept your supervisor/manager informed.

Example

'Every job has its problems, of course. In [the sort of work you do] common difficulties include [mention some of the everyday practical difficulties that crop up in your job – breakdowns, malfunctions, hold-ups]. My supervisor relies on me to resolve everyday problems in the course of the work. For example, [give an example of how you resolved one of these problems – choose something that displays the points set out above]. On another occasion, [give an example of how you saw a problem coming and took steps to prevent it].'

Q 'What are your views on health and safety?'

The interviewer wants to know if you:

are aware of the importance of health and safety;

know about health and safety issues relevant to your job;

understand and follow regulations;

have any health and safety training.

Cover each of these points in your answer.

Q 'Have you ever had to bend health and safety rules to get a job done?'

On absolutely no account should you ever ignore health and safety regulations. If you've had an experience in the past where it looked as if a job couldn't be done because of the rules but a safe and legal way round it was found, then include that in your answer. Otherwise, just keep off the subject.

Example

'I've never found it necessary to bend the rules, and I wouldn't expect to be asked to.'

Q 'What would you do if someone on your team wasn't pulling their weight?'

The interviewer wants to be sure you can handle day-to-day problems yourself as well as knowing when to refer them to a supervisor.

Example

'It depends on the reason for it. If there were health and safety issues, if they were drinking on the job for example, I would discuss it with the supervisor. If they were just being lazy, I'd joke them out of it until they got the message [for example]. [Tell them about a time when you successfully resolved a similar situation in a way that kept everybody happy.]'

Professional knowledge

As well as the questions above, you can expect to be asked specific things about your current job and the job you're applying for. It's not possible to cover all the questions that might come up; they are too individual. You know your own work, however, and should be able to anticipate what they'll be. They will include things like:

how you deal with actual situations that arise in your work;

your experience of using particular machinery or equipment;

your understanding of specific processes used in your occupation;

how you set about certain tasks commonly occurring in the job;

what you would do in specific circumstances likely to occur in the job.

Give full, detailed answers based on your real-life experience.

KEY TAKE-AWAYS FROM CHAPTER 8

Make sure you know what the Core Question for your type of job is, and the key qualities needed to answer that question positively.

Reflect those key qualities confidently in your answers.

When you're preparing, build your answers around:

- Your practical knowledge and hands-on experience.
- Your competence and responsibility.
- Your dependability.

WHAT THE EXPERT SAYS

Don't try to give the 'right' answer; give an honest one. Because some of the processes can be dangerous, we need people who can judge the situation and act accordingly, but we also need people who can act on their own initiative. It's not really a trick question, but something we do is to ask a couple of questions about situations the interviewee should be able to handle themselves, followed by one where they should clearly call in expert help. Some people have a real struggle admitting they'd pass the problem on rather than tackle it themselves, but that's what we want them to do.

Senior Chemical Engineer, chemical plant

9

QUESTIONS FOR CREATIVE JOBS
CORE QUESTION: 'WILL YOU DELIVER?'

Typical jobs:

- product designer;
- feature writer;
- video maker;
- photographer;
- graphic artist;
- copywriter;
- website designer;
- architect;
- interior designer;
- window dresser;
- musician;
- producer;
- director;
- screenwriter;
- game designer;
- illustrator;
- fashion or textile designer;
- model maker.

Creative people provide solutions to problems. It's their job to use their technical skill, talent and expertise to achieve tangible results with originality and flair. Businesses need to know that their creative people, whether designers, artists, writers or whatever, will come up with innovative solutions, on time and to budget. If they don't, the business will suffer as a result.

The most important thing the interviewer needs to know is: *'Will you deliver?'* In other words, they need to know not just that you're creative, but that you'll be creative *for them*, and also that you'll be creative on demand – within reason.

'Creativity' is a difficult thing to measure objectively. Proof of your *ability* to deliver will largely rely on your reputation, portfolio and past record. Your *willingness* to deliver, however, is more nebulous. Things the interviewer will be looking for include:

a thorough understanding of your specific field;

your previous ability to come up with effective and creative solutions to problems;

the drive and ambition to produce top-quality work every time;

your ability to work both individually and with a team to achieve results;

the ability to undertake action, rather than passive observation;

your desire to achieve results over and above the original requirements.

The personal qualities they will be searching for include:

self-motivation;

innovation;

flexibility;

energy and enthusiasm;

resilience;

professionalism.

Before you get to the interview, make sure you have thoroughly reviewed, and have a clear knowledge and understanding of:

Your career history. Review your current position and the work you've done previously. Focus on your experience of analysing and solving creative problems. Assess the skills you've developed in different jobs, the specific challenges you have encountered and the expertise you have developed through overcoming them. Look at the proficiency you have gained in each job.

Your key achievements. Creative jobs are results orientated – you need to be able to talk about your successes fluently and enthusiastically. The interviewer will want achievement to mean success in both creative and practical terms – that is, work that has fulfilled its creative brief inventively, completed to deadline and within budget, and that has actively contributed to the company's success.

Your key abilities. Practical ability and technical competence are basic requirements in creative jobs. It's only when these fundamental elements are present that style and originality can develop over and above them. Make sure you can outline the full range of skills you have that are appropriate to the job you're interviewing for, and how they've contributed to your achievements. Good foundation skills will help an employer assess the likelihood that you'll repeat your successes in the future.

Above all, you need to know what you are good at. You need to understand what your specific creative skills are; and the personal qualities that allow you to perform your skill to a professional level. For example, an artist's specific skill might be their feel for colour, their draughtsmanship or their daring use of composition. A writer's skill may lie in their innovative use of language or their acute observation of human behaviour. Understand what your own particular strength is, along with the other supporting skills that make up your own particular skill profile. Prepare examples and anecdotes for your interview that clearly demonstrate their importance and your proficiency at employing them.

Understand, too, the personal qualities that support your talents. Pick two or three to focus on in your interview with examples and anecdotes. Make sure they are key qualities that genuinely help you to do your job, and are relevant to the job you want. They might include things like:

energy;

flexibility;

thoroughness;

patience;

confidence;

drive;

communication skills;

focus;

enthusiasm;

attention to detail;

dedication;

honesty and integrity;

ability to get involved;

dogged determination.

Keep all these points in mind while you prepare your answers to the questions that follow.

Q 'What do you know about our company?'

Naturally, you've done your homework and you know quite a lot about the company. Start with general comments and then focus in on your own area. For example, start with the company's key products or services, its mission statement, main sites, etc. Include background history, current plans and future projections. Next, move on to your own area of interest – its position in the market, for example previous marketing campaigns, future considerations. Finish up by saying why all this interests you and why working for the company appeals to you.

Q 'Why should I hire you?'

Treat this question like the challenge it is meant to be. The core answer is 'Because I can provide first-rate creative solutions to your problems.' If appropriate, recap your achievements, your strengths, skills, abilities and personal qualities.

Example

'Because I can solve your [design, website, direct marketing] problems. I have/am [recap your achievements]. I have x years' experience working in [continue as appropriate depending on the detail given in previous answers].'

Example

'I believe I could make a significant contribution to your company. I can deliver [first-rate copy, top-quality artwork] as shown by [recap your key achievements]. I have x years' experience working in [continue as above].'

Q 'How would you define your profession?'
Q 'What makes a good... [what your job is]?'

The interviewer wants to know what you believe the crucial areas of your job are. If you have read the job description, you'll be aware of what they consider the key points to be and you can plan your answer around these, highlighted with your own individual beliefs and experience.

Q 'What can you do for us that no one else can?'

This looks like an impossible question, but all they're asking really is *'What can you do for us?'* Ignore the bit about no one else doing it; it's just testing your self-confidence – as a creative person, you have to believe that you're unique. Emphasize your key strengths and talents, along with your existing achievements.

Example

'I don't know about no one else being able to do it, but I believe I can bring to this job [key points mentioned in the job description]. I am [outline your key talents] and have [your key skills and abilities]. To date, I have [mention your biggest achievements]. I believe I have [personal qualities relevant to the job description]. In addition, I understand [a relevant factor of the job], which I believe would allow me to [make some significant contribution to the company].'

Q 'What would you do if we gave you a completely free hand?'

If you're applying for a creative job, it does no harm to consider this question. It would probably be asked if you were going in at a certain level – head of department, for example – or were being asked to take on a specific project. If you're interviewing at this level, think about this in detail beforehand, as it could be the main point of the interview.

On the other hand, some interviewers are simply interested in the scope of your creativity. To give a convincing answer, you need to know about the company, what it has done in the past, what its market is and what its future direction is. This means doing your homework. Whether you would continue in the company tradition or break out into new areas is down to your own personal style, but you need to able to:

outline your proposals clearly;

explain why you would make the decisions you suggest;

describe how they would benefit the company.

Q 'How do you keep up with changes/innovations in your profession?'

The question is really *'Do you keep up with changes and innovations?'* Your answer would ideally include as many as possible of the following:

professional, trade and business magazines;

online professional groups;

business contacts;

professional associations;

trade fairs, shows and exhibitions;

suppliers and clients;

courses and seminars.

Example

'Keeping up with new [products, ideas, trends] is, naturally, very important in this job. I [say what you do to keep up]. It takes a bit of commitment, but I've found it to be essential. For example, [give an example of how knowing something ahead of time benefited you, your job and the company].'

Anticipate a follow-up question: *'What do you see as the future trend right now?'* Make your answer optimistic, mentioning key developments and the opportunities these present, especially to the creative person.

Q *'What are your greatest strengths?'*
Q *'What are your outstanding qualities?'*

Your greatest strengths are your creative skills and your ability to deliver those skills on time and to budget. They are demonstrated through your greatest achievements. It's best to pick two or three really strong points and put them across powerfully. Stick to the ones most relevant to the job you are applying for.

Example

'I would say my greatest strengths with regard to this job are my [pick your most relevant creative ability], my [pick your most relevant professional skill] and my [pick your most relevant personal quality and say why it's important]. I have x years' experience working in [your field of work] and my knowledge of [a key, relevant area] means I would be able to make a significant contribution from the beginning [or at an early stage]. My track record includes [state your major achievements], which I believe [outline why they are relevant to the company you are applying to]. Finally, I believe my current employer would agree that one of my key strengths is my ability to do the job even under difficult conditions. For example, [describe a time you successfully completed a job to a high creative level under pressure].'

Q 'What are your greatest achievements?'

Creative jobs are results orientated. The final product – video, website, exhibition, magazine, ad campaign, whatever – either works or it doesn't. You need to have achievements and you need to be able to talk about them fluently. Focus on your biggest successes, obviously, but it also helps to show yourself as a rounded person if you can also include an example of:

- recent achievements rather than things that happened early in your career;

- success you achieved as part of a team;

- a time when achievement was snatched from the jaws of probable defeat (especially if it displays your personal qualities as well as your creative ability);

- a time when you helped someone else achieve success (in a mentor role, perhaps, or a back-room contribution).

Any of these will help to show that you are a current achiever, have a generous nature, can work well with others or can function effectively under stress – all good things in an employee.

Q 'What are the reasons for your professional success?'

This may sound like *'What are your greatest strengths?'* or *'What are your greatest achievements?'* but it's actually subtly different. The interviewer wants to know if *you* know how you work. They're looking for self-awareness. If you shrug and say you've just been lucky, although you may sound charmingly modest they may wonder what happens when your luck runs out. If, however, you can give reasons based on real skills and qualities, you will probably continue to deliver the creative goods. Base the reasons for your success on:

- natural abilities that you've developed and enhanced;

- creative skills that you've built on systematically;

- the personal qualities that have formed your professional attitude;

- the support you've received from others – bosses, colleagues, etc;

- the opportunities you've made good use of.

Q 'What are you looking for in a job?'
Q 'What are you seeking in an employer?'

As a creative person, what you are looking for is the chance to deliver some great work. The job you're applying for provides just that opportunity.

Example

'I'm looking for the opportunity to accomplish my best work. My experience at [the company you work for] has shown me I have a talent for [something relevant to the job you're applying for]. I believe that it's demonstrated by [give your achievements using that talent or skill]. I am looking for the opportunity to continue to achieve at that level and beyond, and a company that will help me continue to develop professionally. So, I suppose I would say that what I'm looking for is a progressive company that will provide a challenging, stimulating and supportive environment for its employees and their achievements (be as specific as possible). I believe your company offers just such an opportunity.'

Q 'Under what conditions do you work best/produce your best results?'

You have to be honest about this, for your own peace of mind if nothing else. If you say you relish the cut-and-thrust environment that particular company prides itself on when you would actually find it intimidating, you are not going to enjoy working there and you will not produce good work. Otherwise, go for balance – you're happy to work in a team, but equally able to be a self-starter; you function well under stress but appreciate a harmonious environment; you're happy to work closely with your boss when required, but are self-motivated and independent, etc. Add to this some specific quality of the company you're applying to that would enable you to produce good results.

Example

'I'm fairly equable. I've worked in a variety of environments [mention a couple] so I've learnt to adapt. As a result, I'm happy to work in a team [for example], but equally able to work independently given a free hand. I function well under stress when necessary, but, like most people, I appreciate a harmonious atmosphere. I've found that on the whole I work best when [give your preferred conditions, matching them as far as possible to what you know about the company]. I believe that [mention some aspect of the company you're applying to] would enable me to produce good results, which is one of my reasons for applying.'

Q 'What would you say your attitude to challenge is?'

Few creative people actively avoid challenge; most relish it and find it stimulates some of their best work. You need to get your appetite for a challenge across to the interviewer. You also need to make it clear that, when you take on a challenge, you intend to succeed. Base your answer on anecdotes about challenges you've take on in the past and how you've met and overcome them. Include the benefit your success brought to the company.

Q 'What is your attitude to risk?'

Risk is one of those double-edged swords – you don't want to be considered unadventurous, but on the other hand you can't be seen as reckless. Risk in a creative job is different from risk in more practical jobs. It's unlikely that your risk would endanger life or limb. It's quite probable, however, that your risk taking could cost the company money or prestige. The ideal answer shows you know how to calculate risk and take appropriate action. If in doubt, ask them what sort of risks they have in mind.

Example

'While I would never take a risk that would compromise the reputation of the company, most creative work entails going out on a limb from time to time. For example, [give an illustration of a time you took a risk that paid off. Include details of how you analysed the risk, weighed the options, came to the decision it was worth it, and kept your employer in the picture. Include how the risk paid off – for the company or client, not only for you]. On another occasion, however, [give another brief anecdote about a time you were faced with taking a big risk but came up with a solution that avoided it but was just as innovative].'

Q 'Would you say you are innovative?'

This question is best answered with anecdotes about the times when you've displayed your talent for new ideas, how you made them workable, how they were successful and their benefit to the company.

Q 'How well do you interact with people at different levels?'

You will probably be asked this question if the job you are applying for involves you working with two sets of people with different needs, for example a designer who has to take the requirements of production staff into consideration as well as those of management and clients, while still being able to put their own view across. Your answer needs to demonstrate that you can communicate confidently and effectively with everyone involved.

Example

'I haven't experienced problems at any level. In my current job [or whatever experience you are using if you don't have workplace experience] I have to work with [the different groups you deal with]. I'm expected to [outline the dealings you have – presentations, discussions, reports, etc – and at what level – departmental, board, client]. For example, [give an illustration of how you communicated confidently and effectively with people at different levels of the company hierarchy].'

Q 'How do you approach a project?'

They want to know if you are methodical and systematic in your approach, rather than flying by the seat of your pants. The latter approach they see as unreliable and likely to cost them money and/or prestige when you fail. Tell them how you undertook a typical project, taking into account:

creative planning – how you generate and refine ideas;

resource planning – what you need to get the job done: tools, materials, people, equipment, etc;

time planning – scheduling what must be done when, if the completion date is to be met;

budget planning – allocating money, time and resources to each stage of the project;

contingency planning – what you'll do when things go wrong, including time and cost overspends.

Q 'Are you sensitive to criticism?'

Q 'Describe a situation where your work was criticized. How did you respond?'

Unless you intend to play safe all the time, criticism is inevitable in most jobs and especially creative ones where you have to take risks. The interviewer wants to know if you're going to be difficult every time and make life unpleasant for everyone. On the other hand, you don't want to give the impression that you can't stand up for your ideas. Give an answer that shows you are open-minded and mature. If asked to describe a situation, choose one from early in your career that doesn't show you in too bad a light and where the consequences weren't too disastrous.

Example

'I believe I'm mature enough to handle constructive criticism. It's essential, in fact, if I want to continue to improve my performance. I remember early in my career, [describe the event and how it arose. Who did the criticizing?]. I listened to what they said and [when the circumstances were explained] I could see that they had a point. We discussed it and [go on to describe how you came to a mutually agreeable solution]. I learnt that [mention something that was useful to you subsequently].'

Q 'How do you handle rejection?'

This question, like the one about criticism above, looks at your resilience. Companies need their staff to be emotionally tough, buoyant and quick to recover from setbacks. Not all ideas are accepted and they want to be sure that you will accept rejection robustly and come up with new and better suggestions.

Example

'Unfortunately, rejection is sometimes a part of being a [what you are] when you have to come up with so many [ideas, designs, etc]. Experience has taught me that the next idea will be better, so I just get on with it. For example, [give an illustration of how, after an initial idea was rejected, you went on to put a twist on it that turned it into a success].'

Q 'Have you ever failed to meet a challenge?'

The only safe answer here is 'No'. Illustrate your answer with an anecdote showing how you rose to a challenge against all the odds and the benefit to the company of doing so.

Q 'Describe a difficult problem you've had to deal with. How did you handle it?'

This is a good opportunity to show off. Pick a difficult problem and describe the skills, talents and personal qualities you used to overcome it brilliantly. Don't forget to say what the benefit to the company was. As you're applying for a creative job, make the problem a creative one that shows off your flair and innovation. Don't choose problems that involve not getting on with other people or disobeying management decisions, as these rarely reflect well on the interviewee.

Q 'Have you done the best work you're capable of doing?'

This question is double edged. If you say 'No', the interviewer will wonder why you haven't tried harder. If you say 'Yes', they'll think you've nothing more to offer. Your best bet is to tell them that you've done some terrific work in the past, but the job you're applying for offers the opportunity to do even better.

Example

'I've done some great work [briefly recap your achievements], but the conditions in your organization would give me the opportunity to do even better [specify what they are and how they would improve your performance].'

Q 'What are you like with deadlines?'

Every company fears the person who has a brilliant creative mind, but who never delivers on time. As a newspaper editor once said, 'I don't need it perfect; I need it Tuesday.' Lost deadlines mean lost clients, lost money, lost reputation and so on. Consequently, your answer needs to be that you have never missed a deadline. Include a couple of anecdotes showing how you've met tight deadlines successfully. Include one, if possible, about how you achieved this against the odds, demonstrating your determination.

Professional knowledge

In addition to the questions already covered, you will almost certainly be asked about specific aspects of your work and professional knowledge. It's almost impossible for an outsider to guess what these questions will be, as they are often of a highly specialized nature. You, however, know exactly what your job entails and should be able to foresee what the interviewer will ask. They will include things such as:

  details about specific campaigns or projects – how you prepared, the issues involved, how you overcame problems, the reasons for your creative decisions and so on;

  your understanding of specific processes;

  your experience of using particular equipment, specialist programmes, etc;

  your actual areas of experience in detail;

the extent of your knowledge and skill;

how you deal with actual problems and situations that arise in your occupation;

how you approach tasks and responsibilities common in your job.

Your answer should be fully based on your actual experience. Let your interest and enthusiasm for the everyday details of your job shine through.

KEY TAKE-AWAYS FROM CHAPTER 9

Make sure you know what the Core Question for your type of job is, and the key qualities needed to answer that question positively.

Reflect those key qualities confidently in your answers.

When you're preparing, build your answers around:

- Your track record for delivering creative solutions.

- Your creative skills and abilities.

- Your understanding of, and appetite for, creative challenges.

WHAT THE EXPERT SAYS

What I'm really looking for is enthusiasm. I can train anybody to do anything, but, if that initial spark isn't there, forget it. It isn't going to work.

HR Manager, engineering company

WHAT THE EXPERT SAYS

Because of the sort of organization we are, we appreciate a high degree of interest and commitment in the people we interview. We're looking for examples of how they've done certain things in the past, how they've overcome difficulties, for instance, but we're also interested in why they want the job and how they see it fitting into their overall career plan.

Maggie Fellows, Project Manager, TUC

10

QUESTIONS FOR CLERICAL AND ADMINISTRATIVE JOBS

CORE QUESTION: 'ARE YOU EFFICIENT?'

Typical jobs:

- financial administrator;
- records administrator;
- clerical assistant;
- office manager;
- secretary;
- personal assistant;
- accountant;
- medical administrator;
- bank clerk;
- bookkeeper;
- bursar;
- auditor;
- securities analyst;
- legal executive;
- admissions clerk;
- bilingual secretary;
- cashier;
- accounting technician.

Clerks and administrators ensure the smooth running of an organization. Offices and departments can virtually grind to a halt if their administrative staff aren't competent. The interviewer wants to be sure you'll fit in and get on with the job reliably and efficiently with the minimum of disruption.

The key question they are trying to answer is: *'Are you efficient?'* Someone who is efficient is:

well organized;

competent;

resourceful;

proficient;

capable;

professional;

helpful.

The most important things the interviewer will be looking for in someone applying for a clerical or administrative job are:

organization;

dependability;

a methodical approach;

specific technical skills – the ability to use certain computer programs, for example;

experience in specific areas – data handling, for example;

the ability to work with others.

When you're preparing for your interview, make sure you've thoroughly assessed your:

Key skills. Many clerical, administrative and secretarial jobs require specific skills such as word-processing, language or bookkeeping skills, use of particular sorts of software, familiarity with specific equipment such as a particular sort of switchboard, or knowledge of a specific process. Review all your relevant skills, especially those that match the job description of the job you're applying for.

Key experience. Review the general experience you have had such as supervision and planning that will be relevant to most positions. Focus on specific experience relevant to the job such as payroll procedures, data handling, etc. Relevant experience in a specific field is also an advantage. A computer services administrator, for example, will have very different areas of knowledge and expertise from someone working in personnel administration, even where the basic requirements of the job are the same. As the interviewer is looking for someone who will take the job over with the minimum of disruption, go over any relevant experience or knowledge you have.

Hold all these points in mind while working through the following questions.

Q 'What do you know about our company?'

Having done your homework, as suggested in Chapter 2, you know quite a lot about the company. Start with general points – what it does, background history, etc. Then, if possible, focus in on the aspects of the company that have a bearing on your own job.

Q 'What makes you a good... [what your job is]?'

The answer is your efficiency. Focus on that and add details of what contributes to that efficiency:

  your proficiency in specific skills and/or processes;

  your experience;

  your competency and resourcefulness;

  your professional approach;

  your organizational skills.

Include anecdotes that illustrate these points.

Example

'I would say that my efficiency is the greatest contributing factor to being a good [what your job is]. For example, [give some brief examples of your efficiency including their benefit to your employer]. I have x years' experience of [a relevant area] and am highly proficient at [two or three of your skills]. These together with my [two or three of the personal qualities that help you do your job well] ensure that I can do my job competently and professionally.'

Q 'What are your greatest strengths?'

Your greatest strengths are the same as those in the answer above – your efficiency and the skills and qualities that make you efficient.

Q 'Why should I hire you?'

This is often asked as a bit of a challenge to see if you can stand up for yourself under mild pressure. Show how unflappable you are, stay calm and give an answer that says, in effect, 'Because I can take over the job smoothly and efficiently with as little disruption as possible.' If you haven't already mentioned them, assure the interviewer of your competence, knowledge and proficiency. Demonstrate that you understand what the job requires and that you can deliver it.

Example

I believe that my background in [your relevant experience] and familiarity with [a relevant process or professional area] mean that I would pick up the job quickly and make a significant contribution from the start.'

Example

'Because I have x years' experience working in [the relevant area] and would be able to take over the job smoothly and efficiently with as little disruption as possible. [If the following points haven't been covered in previous questions, now is the time to introduce them.] I understand [choose two or three relevant tasks or responsibilities from the job description that demonstrate you know what the job involves] and the importance of [the skills and qualities important in the job]. These have been essential elements in my current job and I appreciate their importance. In addition, I have an excellent record of [a key skill or quality that you've needed to carry out your work efficiently]. For example, [give a short anecdote demonstrating it].'

Q 'Have you worked without supervision?'
Q 'What qualities do you need to work unsupervised?'

The skills you need to work unsupervised are:

  self-motivation – the ability to undertake tasks and responsibilities without outside motivation;

  self-discipline – the ability to meet responsibilities, deadlines and targets without constant monitoring;

self-reliance – the ability to sort out routine problems and use your own
judgement appropriately.

If they ask you this question, expect to be working without supervision for
large parts of the time. Your answer must therefore be positive if you want to
maintain your image of efficient capability. Even if you haven't done it at work,
it's rare for an adult to have never worked unsupervised and have no experience to draw on. There are sure to have been times in your personal life when
you've successfully completed tasks or projects on your own that you can
refer to.

Example

'In my current job as a [what you do], I often work alone without direct supervision.
This is because [explain why – it's simply expected of you; you have no direct line
manager; your supervisor is working on other projects, etc]. I consult [whomever you
consult] when there's a [problem outside your responsibility], but otherwise I plan my
own workload and handle everyday problems and decisions myself. For example,
[describe a time you did that, mentioning the qualities outlined above].'

Example

'In my previous job as a [insert your work experience], I worked without direct
supervision for short periods of time when [explain the circumstances]. However, I'm
an experienced party planner [for example] and have carried out several projects
without supervision, so I'm used to planning my own work and handling practical
problems and decisions myself. The sort of things I have to do, for example, [tell them
about what you do, bringing in the qualities outlined above].'

Q 'What kinds of decisions do you make in your current job?'

This is a question about your level of responsibility. Most people find they underestimate what they do until they actually think about it, so it helps to go through it
all before the interview.

> **Example**
>
> 'In my current job I'm responsible for everything to do with [whatever you're responsible for]. I consult [whoever you consult] when there's a [problem outside your responsibility – give some very brief examples], but otherwise I plan my own work schedule [for example] and handle everyday problems and decisions myself. For example, [give an idea of the sort of decisions you take in a normal day].'

Q 'Have you ever had any problems with supervisors?'

The only answer you can sensibly give is 'No'.

> **Example**
>
> 'I've never had any problems that I can think of. Maybe I've been lucky with the people I've had supervising me, but I believe that supervisors are there to see that the job gets done efficiently and I understand how feedback and constructive criticism are sometimes necessary to achieve that.'

Q 'What have you done that shows initiative?'

You need to have an illustration ready for this question. Think of a time when you acted responsibly on your own initiative to solve a problem or to stop a problem arising. Remember to say how the company benefited from your action.

Q 'How do you decide when to use your initiative and when to refer to a supervisor/manager?'

The interviewer wants to know that you can balance following instructions with thinking for yourself. Give a balanced answer that shows you can take responsibility when necessary, without acting rashly.

Example

'The company I currently work for has clear procedures for most circumstances and I usually follow those [you can understand and follow instructions]. They also set out clear guidelines about what decisions are my responsibility under normal circumstances and what options are possible [you are used to making everyday decisions]. However, if a situation arose where there were no guidelines and it was urgent or I was unable to contact my supervisor, I would do my best to make a decision based on the facts, using any experience of similar circumstances. I would keep a record of my actions and inform my supervisor as soon as possible. For example, [tell them about a time when you did that successfully].'

Q 'Would you say you are reliable?'

Of course you would. Don't just give a 'Yes' or 'No', though; illustrate your answer with an anecdote demonstrating how reliable you've been in the past.

Example

'I believe I am and I think my present supervisor/manager would agree that I am, too. I have an excellent timekeeping and attendance record, and I take my responsibilities seriously, [doing what it is you have to do] on time and to a high standard. I have to be reliable in my work, because if I don't do my job [say what the negative result would be]. So it's important to me that I do a good job even when it takes extra effort. For example, [give an example of when you had to overcome a problem or setback and make an extra effort to get a job done, and the resulting benefit to the company].'

Q 'Do you like analytical tasks?'

If the job you're applying for includes a high proportion of analytical tasks, then you have to give a positive answer to this one. As above, a 'Yes' or 'No' answer is less convincing than one that offers an illustrative anecdote.

Example

'I enjoy doing analytical tasks. I believe I have [the personal qualities that contribute – an eye for detail, patience, methodical approach, numerical aptitude, etc] necessary for the task, and I've developed this further [say how – qualifications, training, experience]. I believe they are valuable skills. [Give a brief illustration of a time your analytical skills have been of benefit to the company.] I've used these skills [how, when and where], and my decision to apply for this job is [to some extent or to a large degree, depending on your own tastes and the nature of the job] influenced by that.'

Q 'Do you get bored doing routine work?'

A lot of clerical and administrative work entails a high proportion of routine, so suggesting that you do get bored won't go down well. However, implying that you love doing routine work makes you look dull and lacking in initiative. Try to strike a reasonable balance in your answer.

Example

'Every job entails a degree of routine. I'm lucky in that I have a methodical approach to things and can do routine jobs thoroughly and efficiently.'

Q 'Do you like doing detailed work?'

A lot of clerical and administrative jobs require attention to detail. If they ask you this question, attention to detail is probably an important feature of the job you're applying for.

Example

'I enjoy doing detailed work. I have a methodical approach and can do that sort of work thoroughly and efficiently. I believe I also have [the personal qualities that contribute – eye for detail, patience, logical approach] necessary for the task and have used these skills [say how and where you've successfully done detailed work, whether in your job or in some other capacity].'

Q 'Do you prefer routine tasks and regular hours?'

This can be a slightly tricky question. You can't say you don't like routine work and regular hours because that's what clerical work largely entails (see above). However, if you say you prefer them, you could seem to be lacking in ambition and, even worse, such a preference could indicate that you might go to pieces or make a fuss if they ask you to work extra hours or carry out a non-routine task. Your answer has to strike a balance.

Example

'I appreciate that [the type of work you're applying for] largely entails routine work and regular hours. I'm used to that; that's the sort of job it is, most of the time. However, there have been times, as there are in all jobs, when the work has been far from routine and the hours very irregular. I believe, and I'm sure my current/previous employer would agree, that I've risen to those occasions and met the demands efficiently and effectively. For example, [tell them about a time when you've done so, including the benefit to the company].'

Q 'Can you follow instructions?'

The interviewer wants to know if you can deal efficiently with instructions, that is:

understand them;

clarify any problems;

carry them out;

feed back results.

They also want to know if you follow instructions willingly, without argument or resentment. Cover both interpretations in your answer.

Example

'Yes, I would say I follow instructions well [give an outline of how and when you do in your current job or on other occasions]. I listen carefully, make sure I understand what's being asked for and clarify anything I'm not sure about. I keep my supervisor informed at key stages and give feedback of the results. For example, [give an example bringing in all the points mentioned]. Like most people, I prefer to be given reasons and explanations for things, and my current supervisor is very good about that. However, I realize that it's not always possible when under pressure.'

Q 'Would you say you are organized?'

You have to say 'Yes', of course. Back up your claim with a brief anecdote illustrating your organizing skills and naturally organized nature.

Q 'Do you work well under pressure?'

Rather than just saying 'Yes', use this as an opportunity to demonstrate how well you've worked under pressure in the past.

Example

'Yes, I believe I work well under pressure, and I believe my supervisor/manager would agree. I've experienced [mention some situations such as urgent tasks, unexpected events, limited resources, short notice]. My priorities in a stressful situation are to stay calm, assess the situation, assess the resources available to me, decide the best course of action and act promptly and efficiently [or whatever else you've found works well]. I've found that pressure can reveal unexpected strengths, and achievement in those circumstances can bring a lot of satisfaction. For example, [illustrate with a brief anecdote].'

Q 'Do you think speed or accuracy is the more important?'

In clerical work, both are equally important, so don't imply that you would willingly sacrifice one for the other. You are both fast *and* accurate.

Example

'I believe both are equally important, which is why I aim to manage my workload so that both are achievable. Fortunately, my experience and [specific skill] mean that I am able to work at a high speed while maintaining quality. For example, [give a brief, supporting anecdote].'

Q *'What are some of the problems you encounter in your job?'*
Q *'Describe a difficult problem you've had to deal with.'*

They don't just want to know what the problems are; they want to know how you resolve them. Choose practical problems and avoid anything that suggests you don't get on with people or have difficulties with your manager or supervisor. Ideally, when describing how you resolve difficulties, include the following points:

You stayed calm.

You were clear-headed.

Experience and common sense helped you find the solution.

You kept your supervisor/manager informed.

Example

'Every job has its problems, of course. In [the sort of work you do] common difficulties include [mention some of the everyday practical difficulties that crop up]. My supervisor relies on me to resolve everyday problems in the course of the work. For example, [tell them how you resolved one of these problems – include the points set out above]. On another occasion, [give an example of how you saw a problem coming and took steps to prevent it].'

Q *'What would you do if a chatty colleague was interrupting your work?'*

The interviewer wants to know if you can handle minor problems and the inevitable personality clashes without letting them disrupt your work or grow out of proportion. Assure them you would solve the problem yourself without either causing offence or involving management in minor personal irritations.

Example

'I'd probably smile and say I was sorry but I was up to my eyes in work at the moment and why don't we meet for coffee during the break when I'll be all ears [or whatever suits your own personal style].'

> **Example**
>
> 'I had just that problem a little while ago. I [say what you did to resolve it tactfully].'

Professional knowledge

As well as the questions we've already looked at, there will almost definitely be some about your professional knowledge. Expect to be asked specific details about the practical aspects of your job. Although it's not possible to cover these highly specialized questions here, you should be able to anticipate what will be asked from your own personal knowledge of the job. Expect them to include:

your areas of experience in detail;

your knowledge of specific processes;

your experience of using particular pieces of equipment;

your experience of using different software programs, etc;

how you deal with specific circumstances that arise in the job;

how you approach everyday tasks;

your understanding of the responsibilities of the job.

Give full, detailed, knowledgeable answers based on the full range of your experience.

KEY TAKE-AWAYS FROM CHAPTER 10

Make sure you know what the Core Question for your type of job is, and the key qualities needed to answer that question positively.

Reflect those key qualities confidently in your answers.

When you're preparing, build your answers around:

- Your familiarity and proficiency with relevant processes, equipment and situations.

- Your competence and reliability.

- Your efficient professionalism.

WHAT THE EXPERT SAYS

I know people are nervous so I don't expect them to be word perfect in an interview. If I ask someone about a time they've displayed a certain skill, personal effectiveness, perhaps, and nothing comes readily to mind, I don't mind if they say, 'I can't think of a good example at the moment; can I come back to that later?' Don't be afraid to go back to previous questions, and don't be afraid to change or correct anything you've said, either. It's better than giving the wrong impression.

Robert Johnson, Area Director, ACAS South West

WHAT THE EXPERT SAYS

I'd rather someone said 'Sorry, that's outside my area of experience,' so I can go on to a back-up question, rather than waffle on and waste those valuable 45 minutes.

Janet Hembry, Head of Education and Skills Policy,
Government Office for the South West

11

QUESTIONS FOR SALES AND MARKETING JOBS
CORE QUESTION: 'CAN YOU SELL?'

Typical jobs:

   sales;

   telesales;

   retail;

   marketing;

   media sales;

   insurance sales;

   financial marketing;

   public relations;

   recruitment;

   sales trainer;

   advertising sales;

   technical sales;

   export sales;

   sales agent.

People actively dealing with the public might want to look at Chapter 14, too. Media and marketing people might find some of the questions in Chapter 9 useful.

Sales people ensure that a company sells its products and makes a profit. The key skill the interviewer is looking for is, quite simply: *'Can you sell?'*

The qualities that most interviewers want in the people they interview for sales jobs include:

the ability to sell;

energy, commitment and enthusiasm;

tenacity and perseverance;

competence and integrity;

the ability to get on with others.

You need to be able to get across the certainty that you will be able to sell this company's goods or services and increase its profits. The clearest way of doing so is to emphasize your success in doing this for your current and previous employers. Therefore, before the interview make sure you review:

Your key achievements. Make sure you have plenty of anecdotes illustrating each of your achievements – meeting or exceeding targets, contributing to increased turnover and profits, increasing orders, winning new customers, increasing repeat orders, etc. Where possible, put facts and figures to your successes, emphasizing your benefit to the company bottom line.

Your career history. Remind yourself of the areas you have covered in the past and the sort of experience you've had. Experience outside sales but relevant to the job you're applying for can be very useful – companies know that buyers like to feel they are talking to someone who speaks their language.

Build your success story as you think about your answers to the following questions.

Q *'What do you know about our company?'*

For this sort of job, you really do need to know a lot, especially about the markets and products you will be dealing with if appointed. Ideally, read the catalogue or product/service guide when you apply for the post as well as getting a broader perspective from the company website, company report, etc (see Chapter 2). Think about what you read and prepare a short but comprehensive outline, ending up with why the company and its product or service interest you, and why you want to work there.

Q 'What do you think the key trends in the industry are?'

You need to be up to date with what's happening in your field to be able to answer this one. Sales can be very sensitive to market changes. Keep an eye on the trade journals, marketing magazines, etc (see Chapter 2), as well as the newspapers. Outline the key trends as you see them, keeping your views optimistic and focusing on the opportunities these developments offer.

Q 'What are you looking for in a job?'

Most sales people are looking for challenge and opportunity. Think in terms of what you can give rather than what you can get – the challenge of increasing orders and exceeding targets, the opportunity to make sales and increase profits as well as earning commission.

Example

'I'm looking for the opportunity to make sales. My experience at [the company you currently work for] has shown me that I have a talent for [what you do – sales, marketing, telesales, etc]. I believe that's clearly demonstrated by [your main sales achievements]. I'm looking for the opportunity to continue to achieve success at that level and beyond, in a company with a first-rate product/service [or whatever the key attraction is for you] that will give me the support to develop professionally. I believe your company offers just such an opportunity.'

Q 'What are your greatest achievements?'

The interviewer is inviting you to make your sales pitch; don't let them down. Pick three or four of your biggest successes to go into in detail, backed up by a couple of others that show your range. Sales jobs are result orientated, so keep your achievements sales based and emphasize the benefits to the company, quoting actual figures wherever possible.

Q 'What are your outstanding qualities?'
Q 'What are your greatest strengths?'

The interviewer is chiefly interested in the strengths and qualities that will be of use in the job. Your greatest strength is your ability to sell, of course. Your outstanding qualities are the personal characteristics that contribute to that ability. They often include qualities or skills such as:

energy;

enthusiasm;

perseverance;

drive;

initiative;

confidence;

integrity;

communication skills;

attention to detail;

reliability;

diplomacy;

interpersonal skills;

determination;

industry knowledge;

approachability;

product knowledge.

Example

'I would say my greatest strength is my ability to sell. I have experience in [outline some specifics – types of sales, specific sales skills, etc]. Within the past [couple of years, few months] I have [give some brief examples of your achievements]. I believe this was possible because of my [pick your most relevant sales ability], my [pick your most relevant professional skill] and my [pick a couple of your most relevant personal qualities].'

Example

'I have x years' experience working in [your field of work] and my knowledge of [a key relevant knowledge, product or market area] means that I would be able to make a significant contribution from the beginning. I am [outline your chief abilities] and because of that I have [give your key achievements]. I believe my current/previous employer would agree that one of my key strengths is my ability to do the job even under difficult conditions. For example, [describe a time you succeeded under difficulties and the benefit to the company that resulted].'

Q 'What are the reasons for your success in this profession?'

Q 'What makes you a good... [what your job is]?'

Give solid reasons. The job description will indicate what the company you are applying to thinks some of the key factors are, and you can also include:

your specific sales skills;

your experience and proficiency;

your competence and resourcefulness;

your professional approach.

Example

'I would say my experience and proficiency make me a good salesperson. I have x years in [your field of work] and am experienced/have experience in [outline some specifics – types of sales, specific sales skills, etc]. My knowledge of [insert a key, relevant knowledge, product or market area] means that I can make a significant contribution to your company from the beginning. Finally, I believe my current/ previous employer would agree that one of the reasons for my success is my ability to do the job even under difficult conditions/pressure. For example, [describe a time you succeeded against the odds. Don't forget to include the benefit to the company].'

Q 'What can you do for us that no one else can?'

If you ignore the bit about no one else doing it, this question is simply asking *'What can you do for us?'* Emphasize your achievements and your key selling strengths and qualities.

Example

'I don't know about no one else being able to do it, but I believe I am [outline your key strengths] and have [insert your key abilities]. To date, I have [mention your biggest achievements]. I believe I can bring to this job [key requirements mentioned in the job description]. I have [relevant personal qualities and/or experience]. In addition, I understand [a relevant factor of the job], which I believe would allow me to [make a significant contribution to the company].'

Q 'Why should I hire you?'

As a sales person, your core answer needs to be something like 'Because I can increase your profits' or 'Because I can make you money.' Think of yourself as a product and pinpoint your key features and benefits. After all, if you can't sell yourself, how will you sell anything else?

Q 'How long do you think it would take you to make a contribution to this company?'

Unless this is your first experience of doing this type of job, most companies expect you to be doing a reasonable job within a few weeks and making a significant contribution with some substantial achievement within the first six months. You can say that this is what was expected of you in your last job and that you fulfilled that target satisfactorily. Give details of what you did and how you achieved it.

Q 'Would you say you have good influencing skills?'
Q 'Would you say you are persuasive?'

This question is best answered with an anecdote demonstrating your skill. Pick something with a win–win outcome and avoid anything that might make you look devious.

Q 'Are you a leader or a follower?'

This question isn't as easy as it first looks. It's natural to assume that they would prefer someone who is a strong leader – someone confident and dynamic with a strong personality. They probably *do* want that, but they may also want that balanced with someone who can listen to customers and be guided by their requirements. Show this balance in your answer.

Example

'I would say that I am, by nature, a leader and I think most people who know me would agree with that. I [give some examples of your leadership skills in action, either in the workplace or outside it]. However, I've found that, to be a good sales person, it sometimes pays to be a follower, rather than a leader. For example, [give an illustration of a time when listening to the customer, being empathic, etc were beneficial. Go on to describe how you used gentle influencing skills and gentle motivation in either that situation or another to make the sale]. So, on the whole, I would say that it pays to be versatile.'

Q 'Are you ambitious?'

By saying that you are ambitious, you are suggesting that you are hard working, focused, goal orientated and dedicated, but it can also suggest that you are cut-throat and competitive. Your answer should reflect the positive qualities.

Example

'Yes, I would certainly say I am ambitious. I have the drive, enthusiasm and [add your own qualities] to make a significant contribution to the company I work for. For example, [give an anecdote that demonstrates your ambition in a favourable way – overcoming difficulties to achieve a goal, for example, either in the workplace or outside it]. I'm very clear about where I want to be and what I want to do.'

Q 'Would you say you are determined?'

They're asking if you will become demoralized and give up in the face of discouragement and rejection – everyday situations in most sales environments. Answer this question with a couple of anecdotes that demonstrate your determination in action. One of them should be from the workplace, but you could also include something from outside work if this illustrates your determination better. Make the outcome one worth the effort, and don't forget to include the benefit to the company in the work-related situation.

Q 'How do you rate your confidence?'

You have to be able to rate it highly without coming over as smug or bumptious. This is possible if you give sound reasons for your confidence.

Example

'I would say that I'm a confident person. I'm certainly confident of my ability to sell, and that confidence is based on my [pick your most relevant sales ability], my [your most relevant professional skill] and my [your most relevant personal qualities]. Within the past [couple of years, few months] I have [give some examples of your achievements]. I believe [outline briefly how your qualities have contributed to these successes]. Having worked x years in [your field of work], I believe my confidence to be well founded on experience.'

Q 'What is your attitude to challenge?'
Q 'What's the biggest challenge you've faced?'

You need an appetite for challenge in sales jobs. You also need to make it clear that, when you take on a challenge, you intend to succeed. Base your answer on anecdotes about challenges you've taken on in the past and how you've met and overcome them. Include the benefit your success brought to the company.

Q 'What is your attitude to risk?'

This is not an easy question. One person's calculated risk is another's reckless behaviour. Risk in a sales job is different from risk in more practical jobs, though, and it's unlikely that any risk you take would physically endanger anyone. However, it's quite probable that your risk taking could cost the company money or reputation. The ideal answer shows you know how to calculate risk and take appropriate action. If in doubt, ask them what sort of risks they have in mind.

Example

'While I would never take a risk that would compromise the reputation of the company, I'll admit I've had to go out on a limb from time to time. For example, [give an illustration of a time you took a risk that paid off. Include details of how you analysed the risk, weighed the options, came to the decision it was worth it, and kept your employer in the picture. Include how the risk paid off – for the company or client, not just for you]. On another occasion, however, [give another brief anecdote about a time you were faced with taking a big risk but came up with a solution that avoided it but was just as successful].'

Q 'This job needs someone passionate about business improvement. Does that describe you?'

Sales and marketing are key factors in business expansion. The interviewer wants to know you appreciate that and can take on the responsibility for ensuring, as far as you are able, that the company does more business this year than it did last; that customers return year after year; that customers recommend the product to others; that the company opens new markets and that it reaches more clients. The key words are 'passion' and 'improvement'. Let your enthusiasm show as you tell them about the improvements you've made in the past to sales figures, customer retention, company reputation, etc. Include actual figures where possible.

Q 'How do you handle rejection?'

Rejection is a common occurrence in sales. The interviewer wants to know if you're robust enough to bounce back quickly and without a loss of confidence or self-esteem that will damage your effectiveness. A good answer shows that you accept rejection as part of the job without taking it personally and, in fact, it just makes you more determined.

Example

'Rejection is simply part of the job; some people simply don't want what I'm selling, I don't take it personally. If anything, it makes me more determined. For example, [give an anecdote where you were rejected and it made you more determined to succeed. If possible, describe how it made a positive difference – made you look for a new market or new clients, change your approach, or maybe even how you tried a new approach with the same client and were successful].'

Q 'How do you handle tension?'
Q 'How do you deal with pressure?'

Selling is often a stressful job. Companies want sales people with drive and enthusiasm, but they don't want people who are going to crack up with stress. At a time when workers are suing employers for stress-related illness, the interviewer wants to know that you are stress-hardy and able to look after yourself.

Example

'I've always been good with stress. Even during exams at school/college, I was the one who stayed calm. I believe it's because I'm good at planning and organizing. I [describe some of the things you do to organize your work and schedules]. It means the practical things rarely get on top of me or drag me down, which leaves me free to put all my energy into [the most important part of the job, face-to-face selling, for example]. I think I need a degree of tension to focus me anyway. I like to feel that tingle [or however you would describe it] when I [go in to see a client, meet a customer, pick up the phone, etc]. Life would be flat without that.'

Q 'Have you ever failed to reach your target?'

If you did, it was long ago, you didn't have the skill and experience you've got now and there were extenuating circumstances. Follow up with how you or your behaviour changed as a result.

Example

'I successfully meet all my current targets, but I remember, when I first started with [an early employer], I didn't have the experience I have now and I came close to missing my targets once or twice. I had to [describe the extra efforts you had to go through to meet them]. I learnt as a result to [include something you learnt – how to plan your time, how to focus your efforts, not to procrastinate].'

Q 'When was the last time you felt angry?'
Q 'Do you ever lose your temper?'

If you lose your temper with a colleague, you'll cause friction and unpleasantness. Lose your temper with a client and you could lose the company thousands of pounds, not just for that order but from any order they might have placed in the future, the orders from people they've told about your outburst and so on. Reassure the interviewer that you are not the sort of person who ever loses their temper.

Example

'Oh, I get angry about [something reasonable but slightly vague – world hunger or injustice, for example], just like everyone else, but I can't say that everyday pressures affect me much. I can't remember the last time I actually lost my temper.'

Q 'How many hours a week would you say you work currently?'

You need to balance your answer between putting in enough hours to get the sales and heading for a breakdown from overwork.

> **Example**
>
> 'It's variable. I put in the time that it takes to meet my targets and my own high standards. I plan my time effectively and I'm good at scheduling, so I believe I work efficiently, but there are always times when something crops up or you spot an opportunity. That's when it's worth putting in the extra hours.'

Q 'How do you plan your workload?'
Q 'How do you schedule your sales trips?'

Ideally, you want to spend as much time as possible on productive work, and minimize, as much as possible, necessary but non-productive things like record keeping, travelling to appointments, etc. Explain how you achieve this and illustrate it with a typical example.

Q 'Describe a difficult problem you've had to deal with.'
Q 'Describe a difficult sale you've made.'

This question offers you the opportunity to show yourself in the best light. Pick a difficult or problematic sale and describe the skill, experience and personal qualities you used to overcome all the hurdles successfully. Avoid, however, anything that suggests you have a problem getting on with people or following management decisions, as these will sound alarm bells for the interviewer. Don't forget to emphasize the benefit to the company of your success, along with facts and figures where possible.

Be prepared; the interviewer might try to take the wind out of your sails with the follow-up question, *'Now tell me about a time when you were less successful.'* Have an anecdote ready from the early part of your career and include the valuable lesson you learnt from the experience.

Q 'What do you think is the key to successful negotiation?'
Q 'What is your approach to selling?'

You will have your own views on this one. The trick is actually to have an answer, rather than um and er about it. Good answers currently include something about cooperation, motivation, customer-led negotiation and win–win formulas. Follow up with an anecdote about a time when you applied your principles with great success.

Q 'What are your views on customer service?'

The interviewer is looking for a positive attitude and the assurance that customer service is high among your priorities, no matter how difficult, demanding or unreasonable the customer might be.

Example

'I would say I put customer service at the top of my priorities. Happy customers buy; unhappy ones don't. For example, [give a couple of anecdotes about times you've dealt successfully with difficult, demanding or angry customers or clients].'

Q 'What motivates you in your job?'

In selling, money is an acceptable motivation, which is why so many jobs work on a commission basis. It's nice, however, to be able to give some broader motivation – it shows your depth of character.

Example

'I like winning [for example]. When I do my job well, listen to clients, meet all their needs and objections and make that sale, I feel an enormous sense of achievement.'

Q 'How do you find out what your competitors are doing?'

How do you keep ahead of the competition? Your answer would ideally include as many as possible of the following:

professional, trade and business magazines;

online professional and business groups;

business contacts;

professional associations;

trade fairs, shows and exhibitions;

suppliers and clients;

seminars.

Example

'Keeping ahead of the competition means keeping up with new [products, ideas, trends, etc]. I believe that's very important in this job so I [say what you do to keep up]. It takes commitment, but I've found it's been extremely valuable. For example, [tell them how knowing something ahead of time benefited you, your job and the company].'

Anticipate the follow-up question: *'What do you see as the future trend right now?'* which was covered earlier in this chapter.

Professional knowledge

You can also expect to be asked questions that explore specific details of your professional knowledge. These questions are too varied and too individual to be gone into here, but as a sales professional you should be able to anticipate what the interviewer will ask. The questions will be based on things like:

your detailed knowledge of products, markets, etc;

your understanding of specific sales and marketing techniques;

your areas of experience and any specialized knowledge you have;

how you approach specific situations;

how you handle specific tasks and assignments.

It's possible you may also be asked to sell something to the interviewer to check your confidence and technique – *'Sell me this pen'*, for example.

In all your answers, however basic or practical, make sure you get your enthusiasm and energy across to the interviewer.

KEY TAKE-AWAYS FROM CHAPTER 11

Make sure you know what the Core Question for your type of job is, and the key qualities needed to answer that question positively.

Reflect those key qualities confidently in your answers.

When you're preparing, build your answers around:

- Your track record of achievement.
- Your key areas of experience.
- Your relevant personal characteristics.
- Your interpersonal and communication skills.

WHAT THE EXPERT SAYS

When you've answered the question, stop talking. Remember, an interview is meant to be a dialogue, not a monologue. If you go on at length it restricts the number of different areas that the interviewer can explore in the time available. At the end the interviewer is likely to feel frustrated that they don't know enough about you other than that you talk a lot.

Robert Johnson, Area Director, ACAS South West

WHAT THE EXPERT SAYS

If you look at the interviewer and talk to them rather than at them, you'll see if they're interested or not. If their eyes start to glaze over, stop talking.

David Giles, Resourcing Manager, Westland Helicopters

12

QUESTIONS FOR TECHNICAL JOBS
CORE QUESTION:
'CAN YOU DO THE JOB?'

Typical jobs:

engineer;

system controller;

technician;

computer programmer;

design engineer;

draughtsperson;

applications programmer;

laboratory technician;

biomedical engineer;

medical technologist;

chemical technician;

civil engineer;

systems analyst;

dietician;

electrical engineer;

metallurgist;

surveyor;

clinical psychologist.

People heading large teams or managing projects might find some of the questions in Chapter 13 useful as well.

Technical personnel are responsible for carrying out production methods or processes with precision, accuracy and efficiency. As they are often the most knowledgeable people with regard to that method or process, they are often expected to be problem solvers as well.

Staff changeovers in technical posts can mean loss of money in downtime for the company. The more quickly a new employee can take up the reins, the smaller the loss. The interviewer needs to know that you have the technical expertise, knowledge and experience to do the job and are able to fill the vacancy with as little disruption to the department as possible. As the work is often complex, demanding and highly skilled, the interviewer's main concern is: *'Can you do the job?'*

The key qualities they are looking for when interviewing for technical positions are:

specific technical skills;

qualifications that guarantee those skills;

experience in specific areas;

dependability and accuracy;

a methodical approach;

organization;

the ability to work with others.

You need to be able to generate confidence in the interviewer that you have the competence, experience and technical expertise to do the job effectively and thoroughly. Prior to the interview, review your career history with a special focus on:

Your key skills. Emphasize your knowledge and competence in applying that knowledge. Look at your skill areas and your experience. Put together anecdotes about situations requiring the use of those skills and the benefits to your employer resulting from them. Be clear too about the benefits of your qualifications and training. What do they mean you can *do*, how do they make you more competent in the job and how does that benefit your employer?

Your career history. Experience brings knowledge, competence and proficiency. Concentrate on the areas of responsibility you've covered, the skills you used and the experience you gained.

Keep these important points in mind while you think about the questions that follow.

Q 'What do you know about our company?'

You need to know about any products or processes that you will be involved with if appointed. Find out as much as you can from the company website, company report, etc, as well as getting a broader perspective from industry journals, etc (see Chapter 2). Think logically and intelligently about what you read and outline a short but thorough summary, ending with why the company, its products and its technical procedures interest you, and why you want to join it.

Q 'What do you think the key trends in the industry are?'

Technology changes almost daily, and companies can't afford to lag behind their competitors, so you need to be up to date with what's happening in your field. Keep an eye on the professional journals, trade magazines, etc (see Chapter 2), as well as the newspapers. Outline the key trends as you see them, keeping your view optimistic and focusing on the interesting opportunities these developments offer.

Q 'How do you keep up with developments in your profession?'

Your answer should ideally include as many as possible of the following:

- professional, trade and business magazines;
- online professional groups;
- business contacts;
- professional associations;
- trade fairs, shows and exhibitions;
- suppliers and clients;
- courses and seminars.

Example

'Keeping up with new [products, ideas, trends, etc] is, naturally, very important in this job. I [say what you do to keep up]. It takes a bit of commitment, but I've found it to be essential. For example, [tell them an anecdote about how knowing something ahead of time benefited you, your job and the company].'

Q *'Describe how your current job relates to the overall goals of your department or company.'*

In other words, can you see the wider picture? Technical people, because their jobs are often so specialized, can sometimes become a bit remote from the rest of the company. Explain the relationship between:

    your job and the department;

    your department and other departments;

    your department and the company as a whole.

Explain how your job goals contribute to the company's goals and how you perceive they fit into the company vision and, where appropriate, mission statement.

Q *'How do you keep aware of what's happening in other departments?'*

Give a brief description of what you do to keep yourself aware of the bigger picture within your company and how you maintain communication through things such as:

    newsletters;

    internal memos;

    departmental and interdepartmental meetings.

Q *'Do you like analytical tasks?'*

Q *'Would you say you have good analytical skills?'*

Not uncommonly in technical jobs, the post you've applied for includes a high proportion of analytical tasks, so you have to give a positive answer to this question. A simple 'Yes' is less convincing, though, than an answer that offers a descriptive anecdote.

Example

'I enjoy doing analytical tasks. I believe I have [the personal qualities that contribute – eye for detail, patience, methodical approach, numerical aptitude, etc], and I've developed this further by [training, experience]. I believe they are valuable skills; [give a brief anecdote about a time your analytical skills were of benefit to the company]. My decision to apply for this job is [to some extent, to a large degree, depending on your own tastes and the nature of the job] influenced by that.'

Q 'What are your qualifications for this job?'

Give the interviewer an outline of your relevant qualifications and then follow up with your experience, which shows your qualifications in use.

Example

'I have [give your key qualifications]. I also have [relevant in-work training] and [any training you've undertaken on your own behalf]. This means that [explain why these mean you can do the job and why they are of benefit to the company]. In addition to my qualifications, I also have [give your relevant experience]. Because of this experience, I have a [thorough, working or practical] knowledge of [a relevant area, process, technology] and am familiar with [another relevant area or process], which means that [show how this makes you suitable for the job, and how the company will benefit].'

Q 'What makes you a good... [what your job is]?'

The answer is your thorough knowledge of whatever your field is. Focus on that and add details of what contributes to it:

  your experience in specific areas;

  your proficiency in specific skills and/or processes;

  the personal qualities that allow you to exercise those skills effectively;

  your problem-solving abilities;

  your qualifications and training;

  your competence and resourcefulness, reliability and precision;

  your methodical, organized approach.

Include anecdotes that illustrate these points.

Example

'I would say I am a good [what your job is] because I know [your relevant area] inside out owing to [your training] and [outline your experience]. For example, [give a couple of anecdotes about using the depth and breadth of your knowledge to solve problems, and the benefit to your employer].'

Example

'I have x years' experience of [relevant area in which you have experience] and am highly proficient in [two or three of your major skills]. These together with my [two or three of the personal qualities that help you do your job well] ensure that I can do my job thoroughly and expertly. For example, [give a relevant illustration].'

Q 'What are the crucial aspects of your job?'
Q 'How do you define doing a good job in your profession?'

The interviewer is asking what your key tasks and responsibilities are and if you know what your performance indicators are. They also want to know if they are at the forefront of your mind when working. Give the standard criteria you are expected to work to and then follow these up with a more personal definition.

Example

'The most important part of my job is [your key tasks and responsibilities]. The standard performance indicator in [an engineering project, for example] is getting the project complete on time, within budget and to the standard outlined in the project documentation. For me, doing a good job means [give your personal criteria for success].'

Q 'Why should I hire you?'

The basis of a good answer might be 'Because I know [xyz] inside out and have an excellent track record of [whatever is important in your job – technical solutions, business solutions, problem solving, etc].' Clarify with specific, relevant details.

Q 'What are your greatest strengths?'
Q 'What are your outstanding qualities?'

Your greatest strengths are your technical skills and your ability to use those skills to solve problems and complete projects on time and to budget. Pick a couple of really strong points and put them across powerfully. Choose the ones most relevant to the job you are applying for.

Example

'I believe my greatest strengths are my technical skills and my ability to use those skills to solve problems and complete projects on time and to budget. For example, [tell them what you've achieved in the past].'

Example

'I would say my greatest strengths with regard to this job are my [pick your most relevant technical skill], my experience in [most relevant experience] and my [your most relevant personal quality and say why it is important]. I have x years' experience, and my knowledge of [a key, relevant knowledge area] and familiarity with [a relevant process, technology, etc] mean that I would be able to make a significant contribution from the beginning. I also believe my current employer would agree that one of my key strengths is my ability to do the job even when things get tough. For example, [describe a time you completed a job or tackled a problem under difficult conditions and the resulting benefit to the company].'

Q 'What are your greatest accomplishments/achievements?'

Successful technical people have a track record of practical achievement. After all, the product or process they develop either works or it doesn't, so you need to be able to talk about your achievements confidently. Focus on your success in problem solving, but it also shows you as a well-rounded person if you can include brief examples of:

recent achievements rather than things you did years ago;

success you achieved as part of a team;

a time you succeeded in the face of probable defeat, particularly if it shows personal determination as well as your technical skills;

a time you helped someone else achieve success, perhaps in a mentor role.

These will demonstrate that you're a current achiever, can work well with others and can work well under pressure – all positive traits.

Q *'What is your attitude to challenge?'*

Think of your answer in terms of problem solving. Show how you relish such challenges and how they spur you to find innovative yet practical and workable solutions. Base your answer on anecdotes about challenges you've taken on in the past and how you've used your skill, knowledge and experience to meet and overcome them. Include the benefit your success brought to the company.

Q *'What is your attitude to risk?'*

Challenge and risk are two different things. 'Risk' is one of those double-edged words – nobody wants to be considered unadventurous, but on the other hand you can't afford to be seen as reckless. Risk taking in a technical job can, at worst, be a danger to life and, at best, will probably cost the company money, time and reputation. The ideal answer shows you know how to anticipate risks and take appropriate action to avoid them. If in doubt, ask them what sort of risks they have in mind.

Example

'I would never take a risk that would compromise the safety of the staff or the reputation of the company. For example, [give an illustration of a time you were faced with a big risk and used your problem-solving skills to come up with an innovative solution that avoided it].'

Q *'What are your views on health and safety in your job?'*

Some technical jobs involve potentially hazardous processes or working in dangerous environments. The interviewer needs to know that you:

   are aware of the importance of health and safety;

   know about health and safety issues relevant to your job;

   understand and follow regulations;

   have any health and safety training.

Cover these points in your answer.

Q *'Have you ever had to bend health and safety rules to get a job done?'*

On absolutely no account should you ignore health and safety regulations. If you've had an experience in the past where it looked as if a job couldn't be done because of the rules but you found a safe and legal solution, then include that in your answer. Otherwise, don't rise to the bait.

Example

'I've never found it necessary to bend the rules, and I wouldn't expect to be asked to.'

Q 'How do you deal with criticism?'

Managers sometimes find it difficult to criticize or even question the work of technical personnel. Because technical knowledge can be so specialized, it's difficult to assess performance unless the manager is in the same field. The interviewer wants to know if you are going to be difficult or easy to manage in this respect. They are looking for a mature, open-minded answer that shows you can accept constructive criticism while still standing up for your ideas and principles and, where necessary, pointing out technical aspects that may have been over-looked or misunderstood. Provide an anecdote from early in your career that shows you accepting suggestions and learning from them.

Example

'I believe I'm mature enough to handle constructive criticism. It's essential, in fact, if I want to continue to improve my performance. I remember early in my career [describe the event and how it arose. Who did the criticizing?]. I listened to what they said and [when the circumstances were explained] I could see that they had a point. We discussed it and [go on to describe how you came to a mutually agreeable solution]. I learnt from that [something useful in the rest of your career].'

Q 'Would you call yourself a problem solver?'
Q 'Would you say you are innovative?'

Answer this question with a couple of anecdotes illustrating your problem-solving skills. Describe the problem and how you used your skill, knowledge and experience to arrive at an elegant, workable solution. Don't forget to include the benefit to the company.

Q 'Can you work under pressure?'

Q 'What kinds of pressures arise in your job?'

Everybody has to work under pressure at some time. The question here is whether you can maintain your competence, expertise and accuracy while doing so.

Example

'The nature of my job means that I've had to work under pressure [very often, quite often, fairly often, occasionally]. The sort of things that can arise are [give some examples]. I don't find working under pressure a problem; I've learnt to [say what practical things you do to manage it]. I've found that can actually be constructive; there's a tremendous sense of satisfaction when you succeed. For example, [give some examples of when you worked successfully under pressure. If possible, include at least one occasion when the need to maintain accuracy was paramount, and how you achieved that].'

Q 'How do you approach a project?'

They want to know if you are methodical and systematic in your approach. If you aren't, they could see you as unreliable and likely to cost them money and/or reputation when you fail. Take into account:

    your problem-solving approach to the project;

    resource planning – what you need to get the job done: tools, materials, people, equipment, etc;

    time planning – scheduling what must be done when, if the completion date is to be met;

    budget planning – allocating money, time and resources to each stage of the project;

    contingency planning – what you'll do when things go wrong, including time and cost overspends.

Q 'How do you interact with people at different levels?'

This question will come up when the job you are applying for involves working with two sets of people with different needs and constraints, for example taking the requirements of production staff into consideration as well as those of management, while still being able to put your own view across. Your answer needs to show that you can communicate confidently and effectively with both groups. If you haven't experienced this at work, use an example of interacting successfully with different people on a project in your personal life.

Example

'I can't say I've had problems at any level. In my present job [or whatever experience you are using] I have to work with [the different groups you deal with]. I'm expected to [outline what you do – presentations, discussions, reports – and at what level – departmental, board, client]. For example, [give an illustration outlining how you communicated confidently and effectively with people at different levels of the company].'

Q 'What would you do if your opinion differed from that of your boss?'

The interviewer is assessing how assertive you are. You may be the only person with the specialist technical knowledge. If your boss is about to make a decision that you know won't work, you have a responsibility to tell them that and suggest an alternative. Can you think independently, and can you disagree and get your point across tactfully?

Example

'My current manager is very good about discussing problems and issues and values my experience, so I always have an input into the analysis [it does no harm to say how you expect to be treated]. If my opinion differs from theirs, I try to find out why – what angle they're approaching it from that gives them a different point of view. I then explain the reasons why I think as I do, and in the discussion we usually find a mutually acceptable solution. For example, [include an illustration of a time when that happened].'

Q 'Have you ever had to supervise people more qualified than you?'

This is a not uncommon occurrence in some fields. If the answer is 'Yes', explain the circumstances and go on to describe how you successfully established a sense of rapport and cooperation with them, how you motivated them and how you possibly even learnt from them in an environment of mutual understanding and respect.

If the answer is 'No', explain how you would go about establishing the same conditions as above, drawing on outside experience for examples wherever possible.

Q 'Would you object to being supervised by someone less qualified than you?'

The inclusion of this question possibly means that your prospective boss is less qualified than you are, so your answer has to be 'No'. Illustrate your reply with any positive examples you have of doing so, drawn from either your working or personal life.

Example

'I did work for someone less technically qualified at [say where and when, in what circumstances]. I don't believe either of us found it a problem. This person was very experienced and an excellent manager and team motivator and we had a very good relationship.'

Q 'Have you written any technical, procedural or training manuals for your company?'

Q 'Are you involved in writing procedures, specifications, tenders, etc in your current job?'

They want to know if you can write effectively, clearly and comprehensibly, so that a layperson can understand it. Ideally, if you know the job includes writing manuals, take a couple of examples of anything similar you've written to show the interviewer. If the answer is 'Yes', show your examples and explain how you prepared and wrote them – the planning, things you had to take into consideration, whom you consulted, etc. If the answer is 'No', find the closest thing you can that shows you can write:

confidently;

clearly;

articulately;

with the reader/user in mind.

Describe any tasks in your current job that involve writing – instructions, reports, operating procedures, etc. Include any relevant experience you've had outside work and express your confidence in your ability to apply that experience to the workplace.

Q 'Have you made any presentations in your current job?'

... because you probably will in the one you've applied for. As above, if the answer is 'Yes', give details of the circumstances and describe how you prepare and how you ensure you give a professional presentation. If the answer is 'No', describe any experience you have had of speaking to groups of people, including how you prepared for it and made sure it was proficiently delivered. If presentations are an important feature of the new job, you will probably be asked to give a short example at the interview. You will almost certainly be warned beforehand, so make sure you prepare adequately. See Chapter 20, Interview extras.

Q 'Have you done the best work you're capable of doing?'

If they ask you this question, they are probably looking for high achievers or people who will go on to be high achievers, so the interviewer is assessing your motivation and ambition. There isn't a simple answer to this. If you say 'No', the interviewer will wonder why not. On the other hand, if you say 'Yes', they might assume you've nothing more to offer. Give an answer that reflects your ambition. Tell them that, although you've done some very good work in the past, the position you're applying for now offers you the chance to develop further and do even better.

Example

'I've done some very good work for [your current employer]. For example, I've [briefly recap your key achievements]. However, I believe that [a specific condition of the job you're applying for] would give me the opportunity to do even better [specify how it would improve your performance].'

Q 'Describe a difficult problem you've had to deal with.'

The interviewer doesn't just want to know about the problem; they're much more interested in how you handled it. Pick a difficult technical problem and describe the skills, knowledge and experience that you used to resolve it. Describe how you approached the problem, the factors affecting your decisions and so on, finishing up with the benefit to the company. Don't choose any problem that involved not getting on with colleagues or management as these simply make you look 'difficult' and fail to demonstrate your technical expertise sufficiently.

Q 'How do you go about making important decisions?'
Q 'Tell me about a difficult decision you had to make.'

If the job involves a lot of decision making, the interviewer wants to be sure that you have reliable strategies in place. Think about how you make decisions and organize the process into a logical series of steps. Follow with a good example of how you used this strategy in practice.

Example

'When I have an important decision to make, there are four steps [for example] I follow to ensure I choose the best possible option. First, I get together all the facts I can. Secondly, I talk to the people involved in the matter and get their input as well. Thirdly, I examine all aspects and try to predict the possible outcomes. Lastly, I try to foresee any contingencies that might affect my decision along with any problems that might arise from it. When I have all that information, in my experience a clear option usually stands out. Taking into consideration factors such as timing, budget and so forth, it's then usually possible to make an appropriate decision. For example, [briefly outline a decision you made using these steps, its success and its benefit to the company].'

Q 'Are you planning to continue your studies?'

Adding to your qualifications is usually seen as a positive thing in technical jobs. It shows that you intend to continue adding to and updating your knowledge. Tell them if you've already undergone additional training since leaving college or university, including any in-work training and accredited courses you've done. Reassure the interviewer that you won't be leaving work in the short term to go back into full-time education, but do tell them of any other plans you have to upgrade your value to the company.

Professional knowledge

As well as the questions outlined above, expect to be asked specific questions about your current job and the precise details of your professional knowledge. It's not possible to cover all the possible questions that might come up; they are too technically specific and individual to the job. You know your own work and area of expertise, however, and should be able to predict what they'll ask. They'll be based on things like:

precise details of your technical knowledge;

your understanding of specific processes;

your knowledge and understanding of special techniques;

your experience of using particular machinery or equipment used in your field;

your knowledge of technical software;

how you set about certain tasks commonly occurring in the job;

how you deal with actual situations that arise in your work;

what you would do in specific circumstances likely to occur in the job.

As your role is likely to be that of problem solver to at least some extent, you may also be given examples of possible technical problems to resolve or at least comment on as part of the interview.

As with all questions, give full, detailed answers based on your real-life experiences.

KEY TAKE-AWAYS FROM CHAPTER 12

Make sure you know what the Core Question for your type of job is, and the key qualities needed to answer that question positively.

Reflect those key qualities confidently in your answers.

When you're preparing, build your answers around:

- Your specific technical knowledge and experience.
- Your competence and proficiency in your key areas.
- Your dependability and reliability.

WHAT THE EXPERT SAYS

Forty-five minutes, the length of the average interview, isn't long to make an impression. I want people who know what they're good at. I also want a sense of involvement and an understanding of how their experience fits our needs and can be of use.

Janet Hembry, Head of Education and Skills Policy,
Government Office for the South West

WHAT THE EXPERT SAYS

It's all a matter of fit. Do your skills fit our needs? Do we fit yours? Ideally, I want *you* to tell *me* how well suited we are for each other and save me the effort of having to dig for it.

Director, manufacturing company

13

QUESTIONS FOR MANAGEMENT JOBS

CORE QUESTION: 'WILL YOU GET RESULTS?'

Typical jobs:

- retail manager;
- financial manager;
- personnel manager;
- operations manager;
- customer services manager;
- marketing manager;
- sales manager;
- hotel manager;
- services manager;
- technical manager;
- IT manager;
- centre manager;
- brand manager;
- account manager;
- production manager;
- estate manager;
- purchasing manager;
- public relations manager.

In addition to this chapter on questions for management jobs, managers may also find the questions for their own particular field useful – sales managers looking at the questions in Chapter 11, for example, or customer service managers checking the questions in Chapter 14.

As well as being well versed about your own particular field, you also need to have specific management skills. The interviewer is looking for someone who can:

organize and run a department;

develop and lead a team;

motivate people;

develop the potential in people;

inspire, lead and support;

manage change;

devise and implement strategy;

make decisions and solve problems.

Managers see to it that things happen according to plan within the company. It's the manager's job to ensure that their staff carry out their own jobs effectively and efficiently, and if not to understand what the problem is, devise a solution and implement it.

The key question the interviewer is asking is: *'Will you get results?'* It's essential that the interviewer believes you will be an effective manager, able to do the things listed above. The best way to establish this is to give plenty of examples of when, where and how you've demonstrated these abilities, especially your ability to get results.

When preparing for the interview, remind yourself of:

Your achievements. It's important that the person interviewing you has faith in your ability to be a successful manager, someone who can make a positive difference to performance. Make sure you have plenty of anecdotes illustrating your achievements to date. Where at all possible, include actual figures – profits, costs, percentages, etc.

Your career history. Whether you are currently in a management position or whether this will be your promotion into management, assure them that you will be able to perform the management tasks listed above by giving them plenty of illustrations of occasions when you've successfully demonstrated these abilities and got results. Your experience of interacting effectively with people, as well as encountering and solving problems, is of prime importance.

Your personal qualities. The personal qualities valued in managers are:

- tenacity and perseverance;
- drive and motivation;
- energy, commitment and enthusiasm;
- well-founded confidence;
- reliability, honesty and integrity.

Make sure you have a fund of anecdotes illustrating the times you've demonstrated these qualities.

Your management skills (or potential management skills). Along with the technical and professional skills needed for the type of work you do, certain other skills are required by managers. They are:

- analytical skills: the ability to weigh up the facts in a situation and make an appropriate decision;
- problem-solving skills: the ability to assess options and benefits and arrive at a solution;
- communication skills: the ability to receive and relay information at different levels;
- interpersonal or leadership skills: the ability to motivate, influence and persuade people.

Again, ensure you have compelling anecdotes that demonstrate occasions when you've displayed these skills.

Keep these in mind when you look through the questions that follow.

Q 'What do you know about our company?'

If you're planning to manage a part of it, you'd better know a lot. Get a broad perspective from the company website, company report, newsletter, product/ service guide, etc before focusing down on your own particular area of interest. Know where the company is coming from (its background and history) and where it's going (its mission statement, future prospects, current opportunities and so on). You should be able to gather enough information to prepare a SWOT analysis of the company:

its *strengths* – what it does well, its past and current achievements, its reputation, positive practices, etc;

its *weaknesses* – no need to parade these at this stage; just make sure you're aware of them;

its *opportunities* – changes affecting it positively such as potential markets, new prospects, changing environments, technical innovations, workplace changes and legislation, etc;

its *threats* – negative changes, competitors, diminishing markets and so on.

Use this to prepare a succinct but comprehensive outline, ending up with why the company and its products or services interest you, and how you can contribute, in a management role, to their future growth.

Q 'What do you think the key trends in the industry are?'

As a manager, it's your job to manage change in your department, so you need to be aware of what those changes are likely to be. Keep yourself up to date with what's happening and outline the key trends as you see them. Keep your opinion positive and optimistic, and focus on the potential opportunities these developments offer and how these are likely to affect your department.

Q 'How do you keep up with what's happening in your field?'

This could be a follow-on question from the one above. Include as many as possible of the following methods in your answer:

professional, trade and business magazines;

online professional groups;

business contacts;

professional associations;

trade fairs, shows and exhibitions;

suppliers and clients;

courses and seminars.

Example

'Keeping up with new [products, procedures, ideas and trends] is, naturally, very important in this job. I [tell them what you do to keep up]. It takes a bit of commitment, but I've found that it's essential. For example, [give an example of how knowing something ahead of time benefited you, your job and the company, allowing you to anticipate and manage change effectively].'

Q 'How do you manage/have you managed change?'

As a manager in charge of a department or even just a team of people, you will need to deal with everyday changes and adjustments to work patterns, targets and outcomes, procedures and staffing, as well as the big, structural changes organizations have to go through at regular intervals if they are to remain competitive. You not only have to be able to adjust to change yourself; it's your role to make the changes workable and acceptable to your staff.

Rather than try to answer it in the abstract, your best strategy is to answer this question with a real-life example. If you have no workplace experience, use an example from outside work. Outline the situation and then describe how you:

- analysed the situation and identified the changes to be made;
- stated the actions to be taken;
- persuaded the people involved to accept change, especially those reluctant or dubious about the need for it;
- supervised the implementation of the actions.

Don't forget to say what positive difference the change made, and the benefit to the organization and the team. If possible, include how you dealt with unforeseen problems and what you learnt from that.

Q 'How would you define your profession?'

Management is a tricky profession; the job title covers so many responsibilities. Read the job description thoroughly to see where the company places the most emphasis – are they chiefly looking for a problem solver or team motivator? Construct your answer around their requirements and perceived needs, building in lots of illustrative anecdotes.

Q 'What can you do for us that no one else can?'

Again, the job description will probably tell you what they *need* you to do for them. Don't worry about no one else being able to do it; the interviewer just needs to see that you are able to match your unique combination of skills, qualities and experience to their specific needs.

Example

'I believe I have the [outline your key strengths and abilities] needed to manage [what it is you will be managing]. To date, I have [mention your relevant achievements]. If I've read the situation correctly, you need someone who [very briefly summarize the job description] and I believe I can bring to this job [key requirements mentioned in the job description]. I have [personal qualities or experience relevant to the job description]. For example, [outline some of your experiences]. In addition, I understand [a main factor of the job], which I believe would allow me to [make some significant contribution to the company].'

Q *'How would you define a conducive working atmosphere?'*

It will be your responsibility, as a manager, to create and maintain a conducive working atmosphere for your staff. On the whole, a conducive working atmosphere is one in which the team is productive. Prepare an outline of what you believe encourages the optimum productivity in your experience. You might include things like:

a cohesive team with a united vision;

clear roles and responsibilities within the team;

clear goals and outcomes;

a degree of independence and autonomy for team members;

supportive management;

positive feedback;

whatever else you feel is important.

The next question, of course, is how you have gone/would go about establishing and sustaining such an atmosphere. This is a direct question about your management skills – how you will apply your:

analytical skills;

communication and interpersonal skills;

leadership and motivational skills;

planning, organizational and problem-solving skills.

Example

'I believe the key factors in establishing a productive atmosphere are [whatever you believe them to be]. They are important because [explain why they are necessary in practical terms]. In my experience, [give an anecdote illustrating your successful use of these factors to improve your team's performance].'

Q 'Why should I hire you?'

See the answer to 'What can you do for us that no one else can?' and bear in mind the core question the interviewer is asking and make sure the clear message in your answer is 'Because I can get results.'

Q 'What makes you a good manager?'
Q 'Why do you believe you would make a good manager?'

The job description will tell you what the interviewer thinks some of the key factors to being a good manager are. Make sure you cover all your relevant skills and experience in your answer.

Example

'I think a good manager is someone who [say what you think is the hallmark of a good manager – can develop potential, motivate staff, devise strategy, inspire the team, juggle priorities, etc]. I believe I am/would make a good manager because of my ability to [pick your most relevant management ability], my [your most relevant professional skill] and my [your most relevant personal quality]. Within the past [couple of years, few months] I have [give some examples of your management-relevant achievements]. I believe [outline how your qualities and skills have made these successes possible].'

Example

'I have x years in [your field of work] and have experience of [outline some specifics, handling both problems and people]. My [skills and abilities] and my knowledge of [a key relevant product, process or management skill] mean I could make a significant contribution to your company from the beginning. I believe my current/previous employer would agree that one of the reasons for my success is my ability to [do the job, motivate the team, produce results, handle problems, whatever your key skill is] even in difficult circumstances. For example, [give an anecdote describing a time you succeeded under difficulties and the resulting benefit to the company].'

Q 'What would you do if we gave you a free hand?'

Unless you are a very senior executive, they are probably not about to give you carte blanche. However, they might genuinely be looking for innovation, and the interviewer might be interested in the extent of your vision, especially if you are being called in to take on a specific project. It does no harm to consider this question before the interview. To answer it, you need to know about the company and the department you'd be managing, what they've done in the past, what their goals are and what their future direction is, which comes down to doing your homework and developing a SWOT analysis as before. Whether you would continue in the company tradition or develop into new areas is a matter for you and your own personal style, but you need to able to explain clearly:

  what you would do;

  why you would take the decision you propose;

  how this would benefit the company.

You also need to do this without being seen to criticize the company or its current methods. It's difficult balancing enthusiasm about both the status quo and potential changes, but if they are looking for a dynamic 'new broom' it could be a rewarding exercise.

Q 'What kinds of decisions are most difficult for you?'
Q 'How do you deal with difficult decisions?'
Q 'Describe a difficult decision you've had to make.'

Management jobs involve a lot of decision making, and this is a two-pronged question. The interviewer finds out what you consider to be difficult decisions; they also find out how you resolve them. Be careful which decision or problem you choose and think of the implications; what kind of decisions will you be making in the job you're applying for? Rather than saying outright what you find difficult, you can hedge a little in your answer. Carry on swiftly to outline how you deal with decisions, and give an example of your successful decision making.

Example

'I've found that decisions that look difficult on the surface often just need more careful consideration. When I have to make an important decision, I use four steps [for example] to make sure I choose the best option. First, I gather all the facts. Secondly, I talk to the people involved and get their opinion. Thirdly, I look at everything and try to predict the possible outcomes. Finally, I try to envisage any problems that might affect my decision along with the eventualities that might develop from it. In my experience, once I have all that information a clear option usually emerges and it's possible to make a decision, taking into consideration factors such as timing, budget and so forth. For example, [briefly outline a decision you made using these steps, its success and its benefit to the company].'

Q 'Describe a difficult problem you've had to deal with.'

As above, choose your problem with regard to the problems you'll be dealing with in the new job, and pick one that shows off your most relevant management skills at their best. Describe the skills, knowledge and experience you used to resolve the problem. Describe how you approached it, the factors affecting your decisions, how you put the solution into effect and so on, finishing up with the benefit to the company.

Having listened to your answer, the interviewer may follow up with *'Now tell me about a time when the outcome was less successful.'* They want to know how you cope with adversity and disappointment. Choose an event from the early part of your career – when you were young and foolish – and emphasize the valuable lesson you learnt from it.

Q 'What would you do if I told you your presentation earlier was terrible?'

Don't worry, your presentation was probably fine – this is a stress question designed to unsettle you. Don't rise to the bait. The question the interviewer is really asking is *'How do you respond to criticism?'* Prove that you are a mature, open-minded individual who can accept and act on constructive criticism to improve their performance, while still standing their ground.

Example

'Well, I'm always grateful for advice that will improve my performance. Perhaps you could tell me which aspects of my presentation you weren't happy with. If you could point out where you feel the problem lies, I can clear up any misunderstandings.'

Q 'How do you respond to criticism?'

As in most jobs, your performance is going to be assessed and this could lead to criticism – the suggestion that you could do something better or at least differently. For managers who are used to being in the leadership role, this can be difficult. The interviewer wants to know if you are going to be one of the difficult ones. As above, demonstrate that you are an emotionally mature person who can take advice yet still stand up for their ideas and principles. A good way to do this is to give an anecdote from your early career that shows you accepting suggestions calmly and reasonably and learning from them.

Example

'I don't take it personally if that's what you mean. I believe I'm mature enough to handle constructive criticism. In fact, it's essential if I want to continue to improve my performance. I remember earlier in my career, [describe the event and how it arose. Who did the criticizing?]. I listened to what they said and [when the circumstances were explained] I could see that they had a point. We discussed it and [go on to describe how you came to a mutually agreeable solution]. I learnt from that [describe the lesson you learnt and how it was useful to you in the future].'

Q 'What are your greatest strengths?'

Q 'What are your outstanding qualities?'

Q 'What would you say are the reasons for your success?'

Your greatest strength is your ability to get results. That's the key quality required in a manager, and it's the point you should highlight in any question asking about your strengths, qualities or achievements. Pick out the skills and qualities that support this ability.

> **Example**
>
> 'I would say my greatest strength/outstanding quality with regard to this job is my ability to get results. For example, [tell them about the results you've achieved and how you've achieved them].'

> **Example**
>
> 'I believe my present employer would agree that one of my key strengths is my ability to get results even in difficult circumstances. For example, [describe what you did and how you did it and the benefit it was to the company].'

Q 'What are your greatest accomplishments/achievements?'

Successful management people are usually achievers. They are, after all, people who get results. You need to be able to talk about your achievements fluently and confidently. Focus on your successes in tackling problems, but it's also useful if you can also include examples of:

- an achievement against the odds, especially if it demonstrates your personal qualities or leadership skills;
- a time when you helped someone else achieve success in a management or mentor role;
- a team success rather than a solo achievement;
- achievements that are recent rather than past glories.

These will show that you are an achiever who works well with a team and functions effectively under pressure.

Q 'What are you looking for in a job?'
Q 'What motivates you?'

Think in terms of what you can give rather than what you can get. Most people in management are looking for the opportunity to use their skills and experience to put their own stamp on an organization and make a significant contribution.

Example

'I'm looking for the opportunity to make a difference. My experience at [the company you work for or the work you currently do] has shown me that I have a talent for [what's relevant to the job you're applying for]. I believe that's clearly demonstrated by [your principal achievements]. I am looking for the opportunity to continue to achieve success at that level and beyond, in a company with a first-rate product/service/ reputation [whatever the key attraction is for you] that will give me the support to develop professionally. I believe this company/position offers just such an opportunity.'

Q 'When was the last time you lost your temper?'

As a manager, you're allowed to get a little more worked up than other professions, but only in the right way for the right reasons. You must be able to remain calm in the face of provocation, but it's important to show that you're no mild-mannered pushover.

Example

'I can't remember the last time I actually lost my temper. Everyday irritations don't affect me that much; there's always something you have to deal with. It's just a part of life. However, I take a very strong line with my staff over [something important – honesty, customer courtesy, bullying, etc]. For example, [give an anecdote about a time you had to tackle someone about this problem. Show how you dealt with it reasonably and fairly and maintained a good working relationship as well as your temper].'

Q 'What is your attitude to challenge?'
Q 'What is your attitude to risk?'

Managers need to be able to face up to challenges and even take calculated risks, should the need arise. What the company doesn't need is a reckless maverick with a thirst for danger. Use anecdotes to show typical challenges and risks you've met and overcome in the past. Present the challenge in terms of problem solving, demonstrate the range of skills you used to resolve it and make it clear that when you take on a challenge you intend to succeed. If in doubt, ask the interviewer what sort of challenges or risks they have in mind.

Example

'I believe that meeting and overcoming challenges is the way to grow and develop. For example, [outline the problem that challenged you. Include details of how you analysed the problem, weighed the options and came to a decision about what to do, and the skills you used to carry it out]. As a result, the company/team [state what the positive benefits were] and I learnt [how you developed positively because of the challenge]. Since then, I've gone on to [how you've continued to develop since].'

Example

'I've would never endanger the reputation [or whatever else is important] of the company, but I admit circumstances have demanded that I take a risk from time to time. For example, [give an anecdote about a time you took a risk that paid off. Include details of how the circumstances arose, how you analysed the risk, weighed the options, came to the decision it was worth it, and kept your employer in the picture. Say how the risk paid off for the company, not just for you]. On another occasion, however, [give another anecdote about a time you were faced with taking a big risk but came up with a solution that avoided it that was just as innovative].'

Q 'Would you say you are confident?'

You want to be confident, not cocky. You can put that across by focusing on how you have earned that confidence and how you have built firm foundations for it.

Example

'Yes, I would say that I'm a confident person. I'm certainly confident of my ability to [undertake the key responsibilities of the job]. My confidence is based on my [relevant abilities], my [relevant professional skill] and my [relevant personal qualities]. Within the past [couple of years, few months] I have [give examples of your achievements]. I believe [outline briefly how your qualities have contributed to these successes]. Having worked x years in [your field of work or specific skills], I believe my confidence to be well founded on experience.'

Q 'This job needs someone who is passionate about business improvement. Is that you?'

The interviewer wants to know that you feel committed to the company, fully involved with its development and responsible for ensuring the company's success. You need to demonstrate clearly that you believe your job to be a fundamental component of that overall achievement, and that you are able to look at the wider picture rather than just focusing on your own narrow goals. Use anecdotes to demonstrate that improving business has always been one of your top priorities and when, how and where you've actually achieved that. Let your enthusiasm shine through as you talk.

Q 'Would you say you have authority?'

A manager who considers other people's views is one thing. One whose staff or team argue with every decision or instruction is another. As a manager, you need to have authority, but without being authoritarian and domineering. Your answer needs to show that you can gain the respect of your staff while still being pleasant and supportive. If in doubt, ask the interviewer if they have a particular situation in mind.

Example

'I don't have problems with authority in my current job. I foster an attitude of mutual respect within my team and I'm certain they could come to me if they had any doubts or uncertainty about anything I've asked them to do. I set clear goals and targets and, where it's appropriate, encourage full discussion and keep them informed of the reasons behind my decisions [or anything else you do]. At the end of the day, though, I expect them to respect my decisions and act on my instructions, and I'm happy to say no one has let me down yet. For example, [discuss a time when you tactfully and successfully exerted your authority].'

If the follow-up question is *'Have you ever had any trouble exerting your authority?'* give an example from early in your management career and say what you learnt from the experience.

Q 'Are you ambitious?'

Demonstrate you have the right sort of ambition – focused, hard working and goal orientated rather than back-stabbing.

> **Example**
>
> 'Yes, I would certainly say I am ambitious. I have the drive, enthusiasm and [add your own qualities] to make a significant contribution to the company I work for. For example, [give an anecdote that demonstrates your ambition in a favourable way – overcoming difficulties to achieve a goal, for example, either in the workplace or outside it]. I'm not saying that I would ever trample over a colleague to reach my goals – that's usually very unproductive anyway – but I'm very clear about where I want to be and what I want to do.'

Q 'Would you say you are innovative?'

Innovative people come up with new ideas and new solutions to problems. Your best answer to this question is to give an anecdote about a time when you used lateral thinking to come up with a creative and successful approach to a challenge that benefited the company.

Q 'Would you say you are determined?'

They're asking if you will become demoralized and give up in the face of discouragement – not a great virtue when you have to lead and motivate others. Answer this question with a couple of anecdotes that demonstrate your determination in action. One of them should be from the workplace, but you could also include something from outside work if this illustrates your determination better. Make the outcome one worth the effort, and don't forget to include the benefit to the company in the work-related situation.

Q 'Would you describe yourself as a problem solver?'

Of course you would. Illustrate your answer with an anecdote demonstrating your problem-solving skills. Describe the problem, explain how you used your knowledge and experience to resolve it and say what the resulting benefits to the company were.

Q 'How do you interact with people at different levels?'

Managers often need to deal with, and be able to communicate effectively with, all levels within the company. They can sometimes be pig in the middle, too, mediating between employees and senior management. Show that you have experience of interacting effectively with many different types of people either at work or outside it.

Example

'I have no difficulty working with anyone at any level. In [my current job, past career, voluntary position] I've had to [give some examples of the people you've worked with]. I'm used to dealing with a broad range of people. For example, [give an example of a project you worked on, for example, that engaged a wide range of participants. Say how you interacted with them confidently and effectively and what the positive outcome was].'

Q 'Why do you feel developing people is important?'

One of the responsibilities of a manager in a good company is to ensure that staff are developed to their full potential, enhancing their usefulness and value to the organization, as well as increasing motivation and job satisfaction.

Example

'I believe that people are the company's most important asset. They are vital to effective performance and success [and whatever else you believe to be key factors]. Developing their potential is an important element in maintaining motivation and job satisfaction [and anything else you think is important], which are key elements in productivity. With my own staff/team, I make sure I understand their career aims, identify the skills they would benefit from and would like to learn, and put together a programme to make that achievable using available resources. I ensure they're supported while they're learning and give them every opportunity to use the new skills they're developing [or anything else you do]. Would you like me to go into more detail about training?'

If the answer is 'Yes', provide the factual details about what you do and how you do it, and then give an anecdote illustrating the success it's been and the value to your company.

Q 'What do you regard as the essential skills for motivating people?'
Q 'How do you get the best from people?'
Q 'How important do you think motivation skills are for a manager?'

As a manager, you can't just demand a good performance from people; you have to motivate them to deliver it. The interviewer wants to see that you have the necessary motivational skills to get the best from your team. Give examples of what you do and how you do it, either from work or in a motivational role outside the workplace.

Example

'I think good motivational skills are essential for a manager. Getting the members of a team/department working together towards a common goal with enthusiasm and purpose [or whatever else you value] is vital for performance. I make sure my team have clear goals and targets, and understand how those contribute to the overall aims of the company. They know why their role is important and how it fits in with the rest of the organization. All the members are kept informed about developments and, where appropriate, involved in discussions and contribute to the decision-making process [and whatever else you do that motivates your staff]. I also make the effort to understand the personal motivations of my staff, be they recognition, challenge, responsibility or whatever. As a result my staff are, I believe, well motivated and work well both individually and as a team. For example, [give an example demonstrating your motivational skills and your team's resulting achievements – excellent productivity rates, high rates of promotion, good bonuses, award-winning team, etc].'

Follow-up questions could ask you for specific details of events, such as *'Tell me about a team member you had difficulty motivating. What did you do about it?'* or *'Tell me about a difficult team member you had to deal with. How did you handle them?'*

Q *'What makes a good leader in your view?'*
Q *'Do you see yourself as a leader or a follower?'*

Managers need good leadership skills, so it's natural to assume that the interviewer is looking for someone who is a strong leader – dynamic and confident with a strong personality. They probably *do* want that, but a manager may also have to be a good negotiator and mediator. The employer might want strong, dynamic leadership balanced with someone who can also listen, empathize and be guided by the requirements of others. The job description should tell you what it wants, so you can show the appropriate balance in your answer.

Example

'I believe being a good leader is a matter of motivation. Good leaders are people who can keep a team enthusiastic and committed to success despite difficult and challenging conditions. I would say that I am, by nature, a leader and I think most people who know me and work with me would agree with that. I [give some examples of your strong leadership skills in action, either in the workplace or outside it]. However, I've found that to be a good manager it pays to be as versatile as possible, depending on the situation. For example, [give an anecdote about a time when listening to someone, being empathic, etc was beneficial. Go on to describe how you used negotiating skills, influencing skills and gentle motivation rather than forceful dynamism to get a result].'

Q *'What are the key factors for a successful team?'*
Q *'What skills do you feel are essential to team building?'*

The difference between a good team and a bad team can mean the difference between profit and loss for a department and even the company as a whole. It's not enough that you can do the job; you must be able to inspire the rest of your department or team to do their jobs as well. Building a good team that runs smoothly with high productivity is an essential management skill.

Example

'I believe a successful team is one where the members are committed to each other and to the successful achievement of a worthwhile goal [for example]. I believe it's up to me as the team leader to ensure that the team is more than just a collection of people working on the same project but a real team pulling together with a strong sense of cohesion. I ensure this in my own team [in the workplace or in some other role] by seeing that everyone knows what their role is within the team and how important it is to the overall outcome. I make sure that individual skill and input are valued and appreciated not just by me, but by everyone concerned. I encourage team members to support each other to complete tasks rather than focusing exclusively on their own responsibilities, and reward the group collectively when they achieve team goals [or whatever else you do to encourage a team spirit]. I also [tell them about anything else you do to support team unity – group activities, group bonuses, social and bonding activities, etc]. I believe I have a strong and unified team. Over the past [few months, year, couple of years] we have [give some examples of the things your group has achieved].'

Q 'How do you prioritize your workload?'

The most important thing is that you *do* prioritize your workload – almost any method will do; it doesn't have to be spectacular. Most systems include things like:

listing tasks;

identifying them as one of the following:

- urgent and important;
- urgent but not important;
- important but not urgent;
- neither urgent nor important;

deciding on an order for dealing with the first two classes of tasks as your highest priority;

scheduling, delegating or deleting, as appropriate, the second two classes of task.

You might also be asked, as a follow-up question, how you decide which tasks are important, which urgent and so on. You need to be clear what your key objectives are, and what your tasks and responsibilities are in order to be able to answer.

Q 'How many hours a week do you currently work?'

This is not as easy as it first appears. Few management jobs these days have set 9-to-5 hours, and your answer needs to strike a balance between putting in enough time to get the work done and burning out from overwork.

Example

'I find it's variable. I put in the hours that it takes to cover the workload and to meet my own high standards, and there are always times when something unexpected crops up. I plan my time effectively, though, and I'm good at scheduling and prioritizing, so I believe I work efficiently.'

Q 'How do you handle stress?'
Q 'How do you work under pressure?'

Management is often stressful, so the interviewer wants to be reassured that you are stress-hardy and able to look after yourself. Show in your answer that, while you have drive and enthusiasm, you're not likely to crack up from stress.

Example

'I've always been good with stress. I was always the one who stayed calm during school and college exams. I believe it's because I'm good at planning and prioritizing. I [describe some of the things you do to organize your workload]. It means that everyday things rarely get on top of me, and it leaves me free to put my energy into [the most important part of the job]. A degree of tension gets the adrenalin going, anyway. I think life would be a bit flat without it.'

Q 'What kinds of pressures do you face in your current job?'

Everybody in management has to work under pressure at some time. The question here is whether you can maintain your competence and exercise skill and good judgement while doing so.

Example

'The nature of my job means that I have to work under pressure [very often, quite often, fairly often, occasionally]. The sort of things that can arise are [give some examples]. I've found that working under pressure can actually be quite constructive. Having to call on untapped strengths and inner resources can be very stimulating and, of course, there's a tremendous sense of satisfaction when you succeed. For example, [give an example of when you worked successfully under pressure. If possible, also include an occasion when you had to keep a team together under pressure, and how you achieved that].'

Q 'What are you like at influencing and persuading?'

Give some anecdotes to illustrate your skills. Avoid seeming manipulative and Machiavellian by choosing situations where you were persuading someone to do something that was either to their advantage or best for the group or organization as a whole. Describe the skills you used to get on their wavelength and outline the benefits of your proposal to negotiate a win–win outcome.

Q 'How long do you think it would take you to make a contribution?'

As a rough guide, most companies expect you to have picked up the reins and be doing a reasonable job within a couple of months, and making a substantial contribution with a significant degree of achievement in around six to nine months. Explain that's what is expected in your current job, and give details of how you have met those targets satisfactorily.

Professional knowledge

As well as the questions detailed above, there will also be questions that ask you about specific practical aspects of your job and the job you're applying for, as well as details of your professional knowledge. You know your own responsibilities and tasks best, so anticipate what might be asked and how you can respond concisely, informatively and effectively. Expect precise, detailed questions on:

your areas of experience in detail;

your knowledge of specific management techniques;

your experience in handling common problems;

your approach to specific situations arising in the job;

your understanding of the responsibilities of the job.

The sort of questions asked might include things like:

'What are the main factors to consider when planning for growth?'

'What conflicts do you anticipate between the needs of the shareholders and those of employees, and how would you balance them?'

'Tell me about some of the projects you've worked on.'

'What methods do you use to predict future workloads?'

'What sort of training methods do you use to develop your staff?'

'Have you used MBO (management by objective) techniques before?'

'Are you familiar with Total Quality Control? Do you use it currently?'

'What software packages do you currently use for project management?'

'Could you tell me more about [anything you've mentioned on your CV or application form]?'

'What type of training do you think is most effective?'

'How do you go about recruiting a new member for the team?'

'How do you make sure meetings run to time?'

'What type of appraisal systems do you use?'

'How do you organize and plan for major projects?'

Give full, detailed, knowledgeable answers that demonstrate the full range of your experience and show your enthusiasm for the nuts and bolts of the job.

KEY TAKE-AWAYS FROM CHAPTER 13

Make sure you know what the Core Question for your type of job is, and the key qualities needed to answer that question positively.

Reflect those key qualities confidently in your answers.

When you're preparing, build your answers around:

- Your track record of achievement.

- Your management skills and proficiencies.

- Your personal professional characteristics.

- Your communication and interpersonal skills.

WHAT THE EXPERT SAYS

Don't oversell yourself. Don't be too pushy, take over the interview or lecture the panel. Be sincere about the skills and experience you have to offer.

Helen Cole, Learning Services Coordinator, South West TUC

WHAT THE EXPERT SAYS

Look the interviewer in the eye and smile but don't be too brash. Don't use their first name, for example, unless they actually ask you to.

HR Manager, retail company

14

QUESTIONS FOR CUSTOMER RELATIONS JOBS

CORE QUESTION: 'ARE YOU CUSTOMER FOCUSED?'

Typical jobs:

sales assistant;

receptionist;

market researcher;

customer services;

customer relations;

telephone helpline;

cabin staff;

waiter or waitress;

demonstrator;

leisure and tourism;

consumer researcher;

travel agent;

travel rep;

hospitality worker.

People working in sales may find the questions in Chapter 11 helpful too. Those with an administrative role as well may find it useful to look through the questions in Chapter 10.

Customer relations jobs are those where the main focus is on dealing with people – the general public, clients or customers. This can be face to face or on the phone, and can mean making sales, answering queries, dealing with complaints or offering help and advice. Customer relations staff are the 'face' of the company, the part of the company the public deal with, and most employers want their customer relations staff to be:

friendly, outgoing and approachable;

confident;

helpful, co-operative and obliging;

articulate;

knowledgeable.

The key question for anyone applying for a job in customer relations is: *'Are you customer focused?'* So the questions the interviewer asks are designed to find out if you:

enjoy dealing with people;

have a positive approach to customer service;

have good influencing and persuading skills (especially in sales jobs);

have good interpersonal and communication skills;

can behave with courtesy, tact and diplomacy;

are calm under pressure.

Before the interview, review your:

Experience of dealing with people. Experience brings confidence. Assess all the different dealings you've had with people, in any capacity – at work or through a people-focused hobby or voluntary role – looking for experiences you can draw on. How have you handled difficult people in the past? How have you established rapport? How have you told someone something difficult that they didn't want to hear? Think about what you did that was successful, and what you learnt from each experience. Build up a rich fund of anecdotes about your actual experience ready for the interview.

Personal qualities. Look at the qualities and characteristics that make you good at dealing with people in a positive way. Gather together examples of when and how you've demonstrated these qualities. Keep these examples in mind as you go through the following questions.

Q 'What do you know about our company?'

If you're appointed, you'll be representing the company. You'll be customers' first contact with it, possibly their main contact when they're angry or have a problem. It's important that you display some interest and enthusiasm in the company by finding out who they are and what they do. As well as having some understanding of their products or services, it's important to be aware of how they want the public or their clients and customers to see them. Take note of the image they present, the reputation they promote, etc, and think about the market they're appealing to. Is their reputation for quality, innovation or value for money? Are they traditional or leading-edge? They'll want their values reflected in the attitude of their staff.

Q 'What do you see as the crucial aspects of your job/profession?'

Your top priority must be dealing with people, and your answer should cover things like:

customer satisfaction;

making sure the customer has a positive experience of the company;

establishing rapport;

listening;

whatever else you've found to be crucial.

Read the job advertisement for what other factors the company considers essential to the job you're applying for (efficiency, ability to work under pressure or attention to detail, for example) and structure your answer accordingly. Be prepared to answer any follow-up questions about when and where you've demonstrated these abilities, so have plenty of good, illustrative anecdotes ready.

Q 'What are your greatest strengths?'
Q 'What are your outstanding qualities?'
Q 'What makes you a good... [what your job is]?'

Your key strengths are your customer relations skills. Pick two or three really strong skills and talk about them confidently and enthusiastically, illustrating them with anecdotes from your past experience.

Example

'I believe my greatest strength for this job is my experience of dealing with customers. I have [outline your experience], which has developed [your key customer-service skills]. It means I can handle a variety of situations, such as [give some anecdotes about some of the things you've dealt with successfully, using skill and diplomacy].'

Example

'I would say my greatest strengths with regard to this job are my [pick your most important customer skills]. I believe I'm naturally [your most relevant personal quality – open, friendly, approachable], which means that [say why this quality is important]. I have x number of years' experience working in [your field of work] and have a thorough knowledge of [a key skill – answering complaints, giving help and advice, etc]. My track record includes [state your range of experience and achievements], which I believe [outline the relevance to the company you are applying to]. Finally, I believe my current employer would agree that one of my key strengths is my ability to do the job even in the most pressured circumstances. For example, [describe a time you achieved success under difficult conditions and the benefit to the company].'

Q 'What are your views on customer service?'

Your views need to be very positive. Show that you understand its value and importance and that it is top of your priorities with anecdotes from your experience that demonstrate that.

Example

'I believe customer service is of prime importance. In my last/current job, 60 per cent of sales were made to return customers rather than new clients [for example]. If they weren't happy with our customer service, they'd go elsewhere and that would mean an awful lot of lost sales for us. I believe that how you deal with [complaints, enquiries, queries or whatever is most relevant for your situation] is crucial and can make a big difference to the customer's experience of the company. For example, [give an example of how you dealt with a situation well or turned a situation around, so the customer was left with an enhanced, more positive image of the company].'

Q 'Do you enjoy dealing with people?'

Clearly, your answer must be 'Yes'. However, while it's easy to enjoy dealing with people who are reasonable and pleasant, you must also demonstrate that you get some satisfaction from working with people when they're difficult, angry or upset.

Example

'Yes, I enjoy working with people; it's one of the things that attracted me to work in [whatever your field is]. Of course, it's satisfying when people are pleasant and everything goes well, but I also enjoy the challenge of working with [difficult, angry, confused] people. For example, [give some examples of doing this, including the positive outcome you achieved for the customer or client].'

Q 'This position needs someone who is friendly and approachable. Is that how you would describe yourself?'

Q 'What do you think makes a person approachable?'

No one is going to say they're unfriendly or unapproachable. You need to convince the interviewer, though, that you're someone customers feel at ease complaining to or asking for help and advice. Illustrate your answer with anecdotes that demonstrate your qualities in this regard.

Example

'I believe I'm friendly and approachable, and I'm sure the people I deal with would agree. I try to put myself in the customer's shoes. I know when I've been on the other side of the desk and needed help myself, I've really appreciated [say what you've found helpful]. I've tried to introduce these things into my own approach with customers. For example, [give an example of dealing with a difficult customer, illustrating your friendly approachability, how you achieved this and what you did to reach a positive outcome].'

Q 'How do you get on with different types of people?'

You get along well with all types of people in all conditions. Illustrate your answer with brief anecdotes demonstrating the range of your positive experiences with people. Make them as wide and as different as possible – mention your experience of travelling abroad, for example, and how you got on with people there, or your experience of working with children or elderly people. Especially useful are examples of your flexibility and ability to learn. Tell the interviewer how you overcame language difficulties to achieve mutual understanding, or how you realized people have different preferences – that older people sometimes appreciate a more formal and respectful approach, for example.

Q 'Would you say you are confident?'

Working in customer relations, you have to be comfortable with people and able to make them feel comfortable with you, encouraging trust and belief in your ability to help them. You have to appear confident. As well as behaving confidently at the interview, the best way to confirm your confidence is to say how you achieved it. Give reasons for your confidence along with anecdotes about how you gained maturity and confidence through experience.

Example

'Yes, I would say that I'm a confident person. I do everything I can, though, to support my natural sense of confidence – knowing the product thoroughly [for example], preparing carefully for meetings [for example] and [other things you do to make sure you're well informed and prepared for your work]. I've always been outgoing and self-assured, and my confidence in dealing with people has developed naturally with maturity. I've learnt a lot, too, through experience. For example, [give a brief anecdote describing an occasion where you gained confidence through understanding, leading to a positive outcome].'

Q 'What skills do you think are especially important when handling people tactfully?'

Q 'How do you react when approached by someone who looks angry?'

If it's your job to deal with complaints, you will need to be able to handle disgruntled customers with tact and diplomacy. Give your views on what you believe are the most valuable skills for doing this well. Include things like:

listening attentively;

using open body language;

taking their problem seriously;

being calm and polite;

being constructive and helpful.

Illustrate your answer with an anecdote about a time when you used these skills successfully with an angry customer and reached a positive conclusion with them.

Q 'How do you behave under pressure?'

Q 'How do you react to stress?'

Q 'How do you handle tension?'

If they ask you one of these questions at the interview, the work is going to be pressured, make no mistake. If they employ you, they need to be sure that you can take the stress without it affecting either your performance or your health. Assure the interviewer that you:

are experienced at working under pressure – saying how, when and where;

cope with it well – saying how you respond, how you maintain your equilibrium and your strategy for managing emergencies;

have sensible methods for handling stress and tension over the long term.

Example

'I would say I'm pretty stress-hardy. I have a lot of experience working under pressure [tell them when and where, including the reasons for the pressure – seasonal rush, tight deadline, urgent order]. I've found it can be really energizing. Having to call on untapped potential is very satisfying when you succeed. If I find myself getting overstressed, I [say what you do to calm down – something quick, simple and effective]. If I know there's a rush [for example] coming up, I [say what practical steps you take to prepare for it]. Long term, I combat any effects of stress by [taking sensible measures such as eating well, taking exercise, etc].'

Q 'When was the last time you got angry?'

In customer relations, you can't afford to lose your temper however much stress you're under or however difficult the customer is being. Reassure the interviewer that you are one of those rare people who never get angry, at least not with customers.

Example

'I suppose like most people I get angry about [something reasonable but somewhat vague like injustice, cruelty to animals, world hunger], but I don't find everyday irritations affect me. I've learnt that dealing with other people calmly and politely is more pleasant and less stressful for me as well as for them, so that now it's second nature. I can't remember the last time I actually lost my temper.'

Be prepared for a more specific follow-up question such as *'What would you do if someone was rude to you?'* Say what you would do to handle it calmly and politely, and give an example of just such a situation from your experience.

Q *'What are some of the problems you encounter in your current job?'*

Q *'Describe a difficult problem you've had to deal with.'*

Q *'Describe a difficult customer you've had to deal with.'*

If your current job isn't in customer relations, briefly outline the sort of problems you have to take care of day to day; then focus in on those that are relevant, such as the ones that involve dealing with people, using interpersonal and communication skills. It's possible to be 'customer focused' in almost any job. If there are people who use your skills or services, they are your in-house customers. How do you balance their conflicting needs and priorities and keep everybody happy? How do you cope with unexpected demands? Include the sort of (practical, non-personal) problems people bring to you, and how you resolve them and send people away satisfied – a large part of customer relations involves coming up with solutions to customers' problems. The interviewer doesn't want to know so much about what the problems are as what you do to resolve them. Focus on *solving* problems.

If you do currently work with clients and customers, or you have a service-focused hobby or volunteer role you can draw on for experience, choose a problem that shows your interpersonal, communication, persuasion and negotiation skills to the full. Explain the circumstances, how they arose, what you did, the positive result and the value to the company or group as a whole.

This is another of those questions that might prompt a follow-up, asking you to recount a situation where you did less well. They want to see if you can learn from experience, so pick an example that shows you doing your best in difficult circumstances but not quite getting there. What did you learn from the experience and, most importantly, what did you do differently next time as a result?

Q *'What are you like at influencing and persuading?'*

Q *'Tell me about a time you had to persuade someone to do something they weren't keen to do.'*

You need to be persuasive and have good influencing skills, especially towards the sales end of customer relations, but in other positions too. Give a couple of anecdotes that show you using your powers of persuasion. Pick situations that show you persuading someone to do or have something that was for their own good or in their best interests, or the best interests of the company or group as a whole. This avoids you appearing Machiavellian and manipulative. Describe how you used your interpersonal skills to get on their wavelength, listened to their point of view, and then went through your proposal, emphasizing the benefits before arriving at a mutually satisfactory conclusion.

Q *'Describe how your current job relates to the rest of the company.'*

They're asking if you can see the bigger picture. Explain how your job contributes to the company's goals and vision. Emphasize the value of customer relations to the company as a whole and explain the relationship between:

> your job and the department;
>
> your department and other departments in the company;
>
> your department and the company as a whole.

Professional knowledge

Expect to be asked questions that explore your professional knowledge and capabilities in specific detail. These questions are too varied and specific to be covered here, but with your knowledge of the job you should be able to anticipate what the interviewer will ask. The questions will be based on things like:

> how you deal with actual situations that arise in your work;
>
> how you handle specific tasks commonly occurring in the job;
>
> what you would do in specific circumstances likely to arise at work;
>
> your understanding of specific customer relations techniques;
>
> your areas of experience and any specialized knowledge you have.

Make sure your answers are customer focused wherever possible, and make your enthusiasm and energy for even the most basic tasks clear to the interviewer.

KEY TAKE-AWAYS FROM CHAPTER 14

Make sure you know what the Core Question for your type of job is, and the key qualities needed to answer that question positively.

Reflect those key qualities confidently in your answers.

When you're preparing, build your answers around:

- Your practical experience of dealing with people.

- Your communication and interpersonal skills.

- Your relevant personal characteristics.

WHAT THE EXPERT SAYS

I need to probe people's skills, abilities and personal qualities in depth. I enquire quite deeply into particular incidents because I want to know how successful they feel they've been, what they've learnt from it, how they've changed as a result and what they might do differently in the future.

Tina M Buchanan, Group HR Director, Hamworthy Combustion Engineering

WHAT THE EXPERT SAYS

I need to know what people have done in the past, not what they think they might do in the future. If I'm looking for a team player, for instance, I want to know exactly how the candidate performs in a team. I don't care if it was at work or not; I want to know when they worked in a team, what they did, how they did it, why they did it and how they felt about it. If they were a good team player then, I can be pretty sure they'll be one now.

HR Manager, insurance and finance company

15

QUESTIONS FOR SCHOOL AND COLLEGE LEAVERS
WHAT TO DO IF YOU DON'T HAVE EXPERIENCE

So far throughout this book, the message has been to illustrate your skills and qualities with examples from your experience. The problem is, what if you don't have much workplace experience to draw on? This is the hurdle many school and college leavers face at interview.

The solution is to make the most of the experience that you do have. It doesn't matter if that experience was gained in very different sorts of work from that which you are hoping to do. It doesn't even matter if the experience was gained outside the workplace altogether. All that matters at this stage in your career is that you have the competencies required and that you can demonstrate, with well-chosen anecdotes, how, when and where you have used them in the past. If you've been asked to an interview, the company believes you have the potential to be useful to them. Your task is to make sure they have every reason to believe you will fulfil that potential by telling them about the times you've done so in the past.

Prepare for the interview by reviewing your:

Qualifications. Your education and training are important factors in this stage of your working life. Be clear what you have learnt, how that has affected and changed you, and how the theory fits in with the sort of work you're looking for. The actual process of learning and studying is important, too. The ability to ask the right questions to solve problems, for example, the discipline needed to study for exams, and the necessity of fitting in and getting on with people from different backgrounds are all elements to be looked at and mined for useful anecdotes illustrating your potential skills and qualities.

Personal qualities. Review those highly employable personal characteristics that we looked at in detail in Chapters 3 and 4. These are extremely important throughout your successful working life, but especially so now at the beginning of your career. They are important because they predict your *potential* and your potential may well be the best thing you have to offer at this stage. Your general attitude, character and motivation are the key to your employability. Remember those 88 per cent of employers who considered good personal characteristics to be as or more important than academic ones.

Achievements. Consider all your achievements, not just the academic ones. Think about any special tasks, duties or responsibilities you've had, and any team or individual challenges. Include anything that shows you as a well-rounded, responsible individual possessing determination, initiative and enterprise.

Work experience. Any work experience will show that you are familiar with the fundamental necessities of working life such as punctuality, following instructions, being responsible, getting on with others, etc. Include weekend and holiday jobs, voluntary work, work placements and work experience schemes. Think about the practical things you've learnt from your experience and how these skills could be transferred to any workplace situation.

When you have little or no direct experience of the sort of work you are applying for you have to rely heavily on demonstrating your highly employable personal qualities (see Chapters 3 and 4) and showing exactly how your transferable skills transfer to the job in question.

Transferable skills

When you have few specific skills, you can still show that you have a demonstrably good range of basic workplace competencies. You can establish that you are quality raw material and will readily gain more specific skills through training and experience.

Transferable skills are the skills that underpin every job and they include things like:

problem solving;

problem analysis;

communication skills – written, verbal and interpersonal;

decision making;

organizing – planning and prioritizing;

time and resources management;

computer and IT skills.

Break down every significant task and responsibility you've undertaken into their underlying transferable skills.

Example

You were responsible for advertising the school music festival, designing and printing fliers for the event and ensuring a strong media profile:

Design and written communication skills, computer and IT skills; budgeting skills and decision-making skills to decide how and where to print and distribute them; negotiating skills to get the best possible rates and also to persuade local clubs and retailers to take as many as possible; planning and prioritizing skills to schedule when they have to be delivered, printed and distributed to meet a range of deadlines; organizing skills to organize volunteers to cut, fold and deliver fliers to distribution points; interpersonal and communication skills to keep volunteers and distributors on-side.

The key is to take these transferable skills you've used in other situations and fit them to the job you are applying for – understand what underlying skills the job needs and demonstrate that you have them.

Explore all your advantages fully, and keep them in mind when answering the questions that follow. Be aware also that the eagerness, open-mindedness and enthusiasm you should display as a fresh, new recruit to the job market are key points in your favour.

As well as reading this chapter, read the one relevant to the sort of work you want to do – practical, technical, customer focused or whatever – for more advice on the sort of questions you will be asked and how to answer them. Although you won't have workplace experience to refer to, you should still, in many cases, be able to base your answers on the examples given, drawing on your school/college/university experiences and outside interests for anecdotes to illustrate your statements.

Q 'Why did you choose the course/subjects you did?'

Try to relate the course or subjects you studied to the type of work you're apply-ing for, as well as to your own interests and tastes. The interviewer is looking for:

- clearly thought-out reasons that show you can analyse and evaluate information and come to a decision – useful qualities in an employee;
- a considered course of action, and commitment to that course, rather than acting on a whim;
- self-awareness about your strengths, interests and talents;
- an appreciation of what education and your course in particular have taught you, for example the ability to reason, analyse, research and communicate, as well as specific theory and skills;
- the ability to match future goals to current action;
- the ability to meet challenges and find or develop the skills and qualities to overcome them – also useful qualities in an employee.

Cover as many of the points above as you can in your answer:

- Describe the process you went through to decide which subjects and/or courses were right for you.
- Outline all the relevant factors you took into consideration – how you researched information, talked to people and got their input, weighed the pros and cons and reached a decision.
- Give four or five specific reasons why you chose the subjects/course you did. Focus on career-related aspects such as what they would enable you to do in the future and how they would develop your natural strengths and talents.
- Describe how the course challenged you and the skills and qualities you developed to meet those challenges.

Use the same process if they ask how you chose your college or university.

Q 'What were your favourite subjects?'

Q 'Which aspects of the course interested you most?'

Pick the ones that have some relevance to the job you're applying for. Don't ramble on at great length, but do speak enthusiastically – you're being invited to talk about something you enjoy. If possible, tell the interviewer about anything you did to develop your interest outside the course and follow it up in your own time. This shows you have initiative, energy and commitment.

Q *'Do you feel your education prepared you for the workplace?*
Q *'What have you learnt that you think would be useful here?'*

Make the most of your educational background, especially if you have little practical workplace experience to draw on:

> Give a concise outline detailing the knowledge and skills you learnt on your course that are relevant to the job.
>
> Explain that being in education has not only taught you specific facts, but has also taught you how to learn, how to pick up new skills and how to apply them.
>
> Describe briefly how your education has matured and developed you – opening your mind, presenting you with challenges, giving you a sense of responsibility, etc.
>
> Explain how it taught you practical considerations such as self-discipline, being organized, prioritizing work, meeting targets and deadlines, etc.
>
> Describe how you developed useful communication and interpersonal skills – getting on with people from different backgrounds, taking part in discussions and putting your points across, giving presentations to classes or groups, following instructions, asking questions, clarifying information, etc.
>
> Include any experience you have working with a team and/or being in a position of leadership.
>
> Don't forget the useful computer skills you learnt.
>
> Emphasize how eager you are to put the theory into practice, preferably in the job you are being interviewed for.

Illustrate any of the points above with brief anecdotes where appropriate.

Q *'What did you like about your weekend/holiday job/work placement?'*

If the job was relevant to the one you're applying for, focus on the elements that match and will be useful in your work. If not, emphasize the more generally applicable things you enjoyed, such as:

> doing a good job;
>
> being part of a team;
>
> learning new skills;
>
> being given responsibility;

working with the public;

rising to a challenge or tackling a difficult task.

Illustrate your points with anecdotes to anchor them in the real world.

Q *'What did you like least about your weekend/holiday job/work placement?'*

Avoid at all costs saying it was boring. You can hedge politely – recap briefly the things you enjoyed and believe will be useful in future jobs and then say how much you're looking forward to getting started in your intended career.

Q *'What are you looking for in a job?'*

You're looking for:

the chance to start in your chosen career;

the opportunity to learn the skills required;

the opportunity to make a valid contribution even at a lowly level;

the chance to use the knowledge and skills you've acquired and put them into practice.

Explain why this position offers all those things.

Q *'Why do you think you would like this type of work?'*
Q *'What makes you think you'll be successful in this field?'*

You need to have read the job description thoroughly and to have researched the type of job. Match your talents, abilities, qualities and training with those required by the job.

Example

'It's my understanding that this job requires someone who is [give three or four of the personal qualities required], who has [give three or four of the key skills and abilities needed] and who has [give the training and/or qualifications asked for]. I believe I fulfil those requirements very well. I have [outline your personal qualities, skills and talents and illustrate them with examples of how, when and where you've demonstrated them]. I also have [outline your training], which has taught me [mention a key factor]. I am sure with the support and training of this company I could make a real contribution.'

Q 'How do you feel about starting at the bottom?'

Be realistic. However good your training, you still have to learn the ropes. The only possible answer has to be that you don't mind a bit.

> **Example**
>
> 'I appreciate that everyone has to start at the bottom if they're to get a thorough grounding in [your chosen field]. So, no, I don't mind starting at the bottom. I certainly hope to work my way up, though.'

Q 'How do you feel about routine work?'

Again, this question is testing your realism. Most jobs involve an element of routine – entry-level jobs more than most. Show your willingness to master the basics before moving on.

> **Example**
>
> 'I understand that quite a lot of the work I'll be doing, if you appoint me, will be routine. I'm not unhappy with that; it gives me the chance to find my feet and get to know the job. I would hope that those routine tasks would become more responsible as I progress and develop and become more useful to the company.'

Q 'How do you get on with other people?'

The interviewer is worried that you've only ever mixed with people your own age, and lack the experience to get on with everybody else at work. You get on very well with people of all ages, status and background, of course, but you have to back up this assertion with some examples and anecdotes.

Example

'I believe I get on well with other people and I think the people who know me would agree with that. I've had to get along with people from all different backgrounds in [give an environment where you've had to do this – college, travelling, voluntary work – and the sorts of people you've interacted with]. I feel I'm adaptable and open to new experience, which helps. For example, [give an anecdote about your ability to communicate in difficult or daunting circumstances – overcoming language difficulties abroad, for example, showing the chairperson of the school governors around, taking a group of under-10s on a play-scheme outing].'

Q 'Have you ever worked under pressure? How did you cope with it?'

You may think it's odd asking people who have just sat exams if they've ever been under pressure, but this question still gets asked of school and college leavers. Remember to focus on the second part, how you coped, rather than on how stressful you found it.

The interviewer needs to know that you:

have experience of working under pressure – outline briefly how, when and where;

are able to cope with it – explain how you keep your balance;

have tried and tested ways of handling stress and tension over the long term.

Example

'I would say I'm reasonably stress-hardy. I have experience of working under pressure [taking my A levels, sitting my finals, for example]. I kept the pressure manageable by [being organized, planning, prioritizing tasks, etc]. I find it very useful to [say what practical steps you take to prepare – reviewing what needs to be done, breaking it down into manageable steps and so on]. I've found, in fact, an element of tension can be quite energizing. Mobilizing untapped potential is very satisfying when you succeed [include a brief anecdote about a time you did that to succeed against the odds. Give a non-exam example if possible – a sport or some other challenge]. If I find myself getting overstressed, I [say what you do to calm down – something quick, simple and effective]. Long-term, I combat any effects of stress by [taking sensible measures such as eating well, taking exercise, etc].'

Q 'Where do you see yourself in five years' time?'

The interviewer wants to know what your career plans are. They also want to know if you have, on the one hand, a degree of drive and ambition and, on the other hand, a realistic idea of what to expect. If you've researched the job and the field of work you're entering, you should have a reasonable idea of the usual career progression and where you should be in five years.

Example

'In five years' time I would ideally like to be [say what you can reasonably expect to be doing]. I think I have the [skills and abilities] to achieve that, especially with [requirements such as further training, experience, specific professional qualifications]. I believe this position will help me achieve that goal because [give reasons, such as excellent training programme, opportunities for advancement, leading company in the field].'

Q 'What do you think influences progress within a company?'

They are trying to find out if you have a good idea of how business works. Base your answer on:

    constructive attitudes such as commitment, positivity, determination, willingness, etc;

    developing your job-related skills and knowledge, and your ability to contribute to the company;

    developing your professionalism – your reliability, resourcefulness, integrity, efficiency, etc;

    developing workplace skills such as teamwork ability, communication skills, problem-solving skills, leadership and so on.

Q 'What are your greatest strengths?'

You have no experience and your skills are untried in the workplace. How can you say what your strengths with regard to this job are? Turn your lack of experience into a strength and emphasize your potential.

Although you can't offer them experience and expertise as yet, you can bring to the job:

    enthusiasm and energy;

    an open mind with no ingrained routines to overcome;

    your ability to learn – you're still in the habit of doing so;

adaptability – you can be influenced and moulded;

freshness – you haven't seen it all before.

Include these points in your answer along with the personal qualities that will make you good at the job.

Example

'I would say my greatest strengths are [give three of your talents and personal qualities that you feel are genuine strengths and are appropriate for the job]. I believe I've demonstrated these in the past by [give a brief anecdote or example that shows you using your strengths]. Although experience isn't one of my key strengths as yet, I do have [give the experience you have and any theoretical background]. As well as that, though, I believe I can bring to the job [go through the points above – enthusiasm, open mind, etc].'

Q 'What have you done that shows initiative?'

Pick up to three occasions where you've shown this useful quality. Aim to give examples that:

show you acting responsibly;

display your problem-solving abilities;

show independence and self-reliance;

demonstrate good thinking and planned action.

Don't forget to say what the resulting benefits were, especially to others as well as yourself.

Q 'What outside interests do/did you enjoy?'

Aim for a selection that covers the range of desirable qualities. Include:

an example of a team activity;

something requiring self-motivation;

anything that has a community focus;

positions of responsibility you hold/held – team captain, editor, treasurer, etc;

something you are genuinely passionate about.

Beware of anything controversial. If you are a committed hunt supporter or hunt saboteur, for example, this is probably not the best time to argue your case. Otherwise, let your interest and enthusiasm come through in your answer.

Professional knowledge

As well as the above questions, be prepared to answer specific questions relating to:

- any courses you've done and the knowledge you've gained, both practical and theoretical;
- details about any project work you've done;
- details of any work experience you've had – what you did, how you did it, etc;
- any extra-curricular activities you've been involved with – sports, teams, special-interest groups, etc.

KEY TAKE-AWAYS FROM CHAPTER 15

Mine ALL your experience for skills and qualities that will be of use in the workplace.

- Look at the competencies asked for in the job and think about situations where you've had to use similar skills, even if it wasn't a workplace setting.

- Look at the skills and experience you have gained throughout your life, and consider how each of them could be made to be relevant to the job you're applying for.

- Your personal qualities are at least as important as your academic qualifications at this stage in your career - possibly more so.

WHAT THE EXPERT SAYS

Be positive about yourself; know what you have to offer even if your examples aren't from the workplace. Persistence, resilience, motivation, the ability to stick at things and put in extra effort are the same whether you've done them at work, school, college or anywhere else.

David Giles, Resourcing Manager, Westland Helicopters Ltd

WHAT THE EXPERT SAYS

Practise talking to people about yourself and what you can do. Many of the school leavers I see can say little more than 'Yes' or 'No'. Getting a whole sentence out of them is an effort. Practise with friends, teachers, parents, anyone. It's not just about the interview itself; I worry how they'll get on with the rest of the team if they join the company. A young person who is friendly and articulate will be streets ahead.

HR Manager, insurance and finance company

16

TACKLING THE DIFFICULT QUESTIONS
HANDLING QUESTIONS ABOUT PERCEIVED AREAS OF WEAKNESS

Once the interviewer has asked the structured questions they ask every inter-viewee, they will move on to the more individual part of the interview – the person-specific questions. Rightly or wrongly, many people feel that this is the most difficult part of the interview.

Having read your CV or application form, the interviewer will almost certainly have queries about the details. They are most likely to want to know more about:

employment gaps;

frequent job changes;

unusual career moves;

reasons for leaving jobs;

being under- or overqualified for the post;

poor matches with the job requirements.

If any of these things apply to you, it will pay to plan your response to the sort of questions that, if you are unprepared, can put you on the spot. You can be sure they'll want to probe these areas more deeply to fill in the details.

Read through your CV carefully with an employer's eye and organize your responses well in advance of the interview. As well as being fully prepared about everything you've put down, ask yourself what questions you would *least* like to be asked, and plan your answers accordingly. If you think the interviewer will worry about something, your task is to allay their anxiety and show them why it's not a problem. Look on the bright side; things can't be that bad or you wouldn't have been asked to the interview. Don't forget to demonstrate your integrity, adaptability and positivity in your answers.

A useful outline for answering difficult questions is:

agree with the interviewer – don't argue or tell them they've read your CV the wrong way. If the interviewer thinks there's a problem, there's a problem;

appreciate their point of view; then add your 'However...';

give your reasons, explanations and/or mitigating circumstances;

give a brief anecdote underlining your case;

confirm it's not a problem that will affect them.

Example

'Yes, [I have been out of work a long time, I have had some unusual career moves, or I do appear overqualified] and I understand your concern that [I might be out of practice, be uncertain of my career path, get bored and move on, etc]. However, [go through any of the relevant points that apply to you from the more detailed answers below]. For example, [give an anecdote, explanation or example that demonstrates your point]. So, although I understand you bringing the matter up, I can assure you it's [not a problem that's going to arise again, not something that will affect the current situation, very much in the past]. In fact, [if possible, show what strengths, skills or experience you've gained as a result, and how that might benefit the company].'

Q 'You were in your last job a long time. How do you think you'd adjust to a new post?'

You can't just say you'd be fine and leave it at that. You need to reassure the interviewer that you haven't become a fossilized stick-in-the-mud lacking ambition and initiative:

If there are good reasons why you stayed on, give them – you needed to remain in the same town; there was a long in-house training programme; it was the only suitable employment in the area; you were loyal to a small company or family firm; etc.

Explain that, though it might seem a long time, the job was always changing, you worked on several different projects and there were always new challenges.

Explain also that you had to be adaptable and flexible in your old job, and give some examples and anecdotes to support that.

Q 'You were in your last job for x years. Why weren't you promoted in that time?'

Base your answer on the same things as above. Briefly mention a reason for the lack of promotion – it was a small company, there was little expansion, you were top of your field with nowhere to go, etc. Outline what you learnt and what you achieved. Emphasize strongly how your job changed and your responsibilities increased even if you didn't get formal promotion. You could also explain that the lack of opportunity is the reason you're looking for a new job.

Q 'You've been in your current job a rather short time. Why are you changing so soon?'

You aren't changing on a whim and you haven't been sacked. Give your reasons and make your case. Acceptable reasons include:

relocation – yours or the company's;

redundancy or reorganization;

a genuine mistake – the job wasn't what you thought it was going to be;

it was a short contract or temporary job;

it was always intended as a stopgap while you looked for the right job;

an unforeseen change of circumstances – you need full-time work rather than part-time or vice versa, for example;

this new job was too good an opportunity to miss.

Q 'You seem to have changed jobs frequently. Was there a reason for that?'

The interviewer is worried that, if they employ you, you'll be off in a few months. You need to set their mind at rest with an acceptable reason and the assurance that all that is behind you now. Emphasize that you are fully committed and would stay in this job:

If you have had a genuine run of bad luck, tell them. Firms do close down, reorganize and relocate – now more than ever before.

If the posts were short contract or temporary, explain that. It might help in future to change your CV so that all your temp jobs come under one heading and it doesn't look as if you keep job-hopping.

Explain you've been gathering a wide range of experience and are now ready to settle down to your long-term career commitment in a company with which you have a good cultural fit.

Explain how you made some bad choices through youthful inexperience but have now matured and are ready to apply yourself (give a supporting anecdote to show how and why you've changed).

Show how the experience you gained in all those other jobs will be valuable in this job.

Show how they all contributed to the adaptable, well-rounded, flexible person you are today.

Q 'You've had a wide range of different jobs...'

The unspoken question is *'Have you found the right career yet or are we just another experiment?'* Again, you need to reassure the interviewer and convince them that this time you're on the right track and you intend to stay. Make your case stronger by showing what each of the jobs had in common and how they relate to the job you're applying for. Show a strong, clear thread running through everything. As most people have natural aptitudes and preferences, this isn't as difficult as it might sound. Perhaps they all use your problem-solving skills or your interpersonal skills, for example. Or maybe they all require a high degree of organization, hands-on skills or creativity. Demonstrate how the skills you've learnt will be relevant and useful in this new job.

Q 'I notice that this job is rather different from your current/last one...'

This is a similar question to the last one, just more focused. Again, give sincere reasons for the change and draw parallels between your last job and the one you're applying for.

Q 'It's quite a long time since your last job...'

The unspoken question here is *'Why hasn't anyone employed you yet?'* Your task is to give convincing reasons for your long period out of work. You could:

Explain that you had an offer that fell through – but only if it was the company's fault, not if it failed because of your reference check or something similar.

If this is a rare job that doesn't come up very often, or it demands an unusual skill, or it's a highly competitive job market and jobs are snapped up quickly, then explain how you didn't want to settle for anything less or take a stopgap job and maybe miss a golden opportunity.

Tell them that in the light of the redundancy (or whatever), you've taken the time to think about and consolidate your career plans rather than just take what was going.

Show how you've used the time to update and upgrade your skills through vocational training or study.

Explain that, at this stage in your career, you want to make the best use of your skills and experience and have been very selective about whom you apply to.

Explain how your redundancy package allowed you to fulfil a dream such as travelling or some other activity and that's what you've been doing, but you're ready to settle down again now.

Q 'What have you been doing since your last job?'

The interviewer is worried that you've spent the time watching daytime TV, have become lazy and will find doing a day's work difficult. Make your days sound structured and full of activity. Include:

job hunting itself – emphasize the organized approach you took to research, networking, applying, etc;

updating your skills – any courses of study or training you've done;

outside interests you've become involved with or had more time to develop;

voluntary work you've been involved with.

Q 'There are quite long gaps in your record. Is there a reason for that?'

The interviewer is probing you. They are not only worried about your work record here, but they want to see if the underlying reason could be a long-term liability – drugs, ill health, major family problems, imprisonment, etc. Calm their anxieties:

Explain the gaps in the best light possible, using the examples in previous questions, and emphasize your readiness to settle down and get on with your career now.

If the gaps really are due to a 'liability', either explain that it was in the past and your life has changed dramatically for the better now (give reasons for how and why) or explain that it will in no way affect your ability to work effectively for them.

Give the interviewer an anecdote demonstrating your current commitment and drive.

For real finesse, show how overcoming your problems has strengthened and matured you and how you can use that maturity in the job.

Q 'Your last/current job seems a bit of a step down. Was there a reason for that?'

Q 'Isn't this job a bit of a step backwards/sideways for you?'

Show how the jobs you've had fit in with your overall career plan, even where that means you've had to take a sideways step to consolidate your skills or experience:

If you're still comparatively young, maybe you were promoted ahead of your capabilities and had to take a step back. You've used the time to mature and develop professionally (say how) and you're absolutely ready now.

Your interests have taken you in a direction that involved a sideways step to develop new skills and gain experience.

You've reached the top in one field and want to bring your skills and experience to a different area even if that means retrenching.

You have new skills you wish to use but need to develop experience, which means you can't transfer directly. You could be a manager going into the technical side of the business, for example, or vice versa.

You're simply downshifting – but you need to make a strong case to show how your expertise will benefit this job. Don't on any account make them feel they're just a soft option or the last stop before retirement.

Q 'What are your career plans?'

This question asked of any female between 20 and 50 could mean *'Are you planning to have a baby?'* As this would be an illegal question (see below) you can ignore any subtext and simply answer the question as asked. Outline your career strategy, focus on your immediate plans, show how this job fits in with them and underline what you can bring to the job. There's a time and a place for discussing maternity leave, but this isn't it.

Q 'Do you feel confident you would be able to do the job?'

This is another question that might have a subtext. The interviewer could be concerned that your age, gender or physical ability would influence your capacity to do the job. Again, ignore the subtext and just answer the question in the affirmative. Give a couple of brief anecdotes showing how you have done a similar job or met similar challenges successfully in the past.

Q 'Do you feel you're overqualified/over-experienced for this position?'

The interviewer either is worried that you'll get a more suitable job in a few months and disappear, or they feel you're too senior to take orders from a younger, less-qualified manager. They might also be hinting that they think you're too old for the job. Assure them that:

You understand their concerns, but you're fully aware of what the job entails and you wouldn't have applied if you didn't think it was right for you.

Explain what it is about the job that interests you specifically.

Tell them in detail how the company can benefit from your knowledge.

Tell them exactly how you could use your experience to the company's advantage.

Emphasize that you believe you can grow and develop in the job and learn new things.

If, after a bit of gentle probing, you're sure it's your age that's the problem, introduce them to the benefits of older workers:

You have a track record of career commitment.

You have a wealth of skills and experience that could benefit them.

You come with a record of success.

You are mature – that means reliable, professional, prudent, responsible, etc.

You're stable – you're not going to shoot off on a tangent at this stage in your career.

You have realistic expectations of life, work and your colleagues.

You've seen a bit of the world and, consequently, you're broad-minded and can get on with most people in most situations.

You've encountered and solved a lot of problems in your time.

Anyone who survived the technological and employment revolutions of the 1980s and 1990s has learnt to be resilient, flexible and adaptable.

Q 'Do you feel your lack of experience could be a problem?'

If they've asked you to the interview, you must have something going for you other than experience. Now is the time to focus in on that:

Use the experience gained in other areas and apply it to the job in question.

Do the same with your transferable skills – the ones such as problem-solving and communication skills that are useful in most jobs.

Make the most of your theoretical knowledge if you've just left college or completed a training course by showing you have a good understanding of how it will apply in practice.

Demonstrate your ability to learn quickly and pick things up fast with a couple of anecdotes illustrating this ability in the past.

Q 'Do you feel your lack of qualifications could be a problem?'

As above, they've thought it worth interviewing you, so they should be willing to be convinced. Focus on your practical experience, the skills and expertise this has given you and how it would be of benefit to them. If the job means you'd be managing or instructing people more highly qualified than you, the interviewer might think you'd have difficulty getting their respect. Give a brief anecdote showing how you managed a similar situation successfully in the past.

Inappropriate and illegal questions

The questions asked at interview should not encourage discrimination on grounds of gender, sexual orientation, age, religion, race or disability. However, the laws on discrimination are complex, and there are often exemptions and special considerations allowed for specific jobs. On the whole, though, you shouldn't have to answer questions about your:

marital status;

number or ages of children;

race or ethnicity;

nationality;

religion;

gender or sexual orientation;

disabilities or handicaps;

membership of legal organizations;

financial status;

spent convictions;

political affiliation.

You can, however, be asked about anything that does have a direct bearing on your ability to do the job. For example, you shouldn't be asked if you have young children, but you could be asked if you would be able to cover night shifts. You shouldn't be asked outright the extent of a disability, but you can be asked if standing for long periods would be a problem for you.

What do you do if the interviewer asks an inappropriate or illicit question? You have several options. You can:

Answer honestly. Give a straightforward answer if you can do so without feeling intimidated. Assess the situation and the interviewer – the question may have been asked out of genuine interest or sympathy rather than discrimination.

Answer honestly and allay their fears. You don't have to, but you can choose, if you wish, to ignore the inappropriateness of the question and treat it like any other difficult query.

Example

'I understand this job involves a significant amount of [travel, lifting, shift work, etc] and I can assure you that my [family responsibilities, disability, childcare arrangements, marriage plans] would in no way interfere with my ability to do that.'

Give a non-committal answer. Just say what they want to hear. Never, ever lie in an interview, especially about your qualifications or experience. You don't, however, have to tell the whole truth when it comes to your personal life.

Issue a blanket statement.

Example

'I can assure you there is nothing [about my religion, politics, family responsibility, age] that would affect my performance of this job.'

Refer the answer back to them.

Example

'I'm not quite sure how that question relates to my ability to do the job. Could you clarify it for me?'

If the interviewer knows they are fishing in illicit waters, they will move swiftly on to the next question.

Refuse to answer. Politely say that you don't feel the question is appropriate. While this is theoretically the most correct response, in practice it's likely to leave both you and the interviewer feeling embarrassed – never a plus at an interview.

KEY TAKE-AWAYS FROM CHAPTER 16

- Be aware of your weak spots – employment gaps, frequent job changes, skills mismatch, etc – and prepare to be questioned about them.

- Prepare your answers ahead of the interview so you aren't caught off-guard, but can deliver a polite, well-reasoned answer that will help to allay their misgivings.

- If you've got as far as an interview, they are going to be willing to listen to your answer.

- Don't let inappropriate or even illegal questions throw you - there are ways of dealing with them gracefully.

WHAT THE EXPERT SAYS

Expect to be asked about anything you've put on your CV.

Tina M Buchanan, Group HR Director, Hamworthy Combustion Engineering

WHAT THE EXPERT SAYS

I don't ask people to interview to humiliate them or catch them out, but I do sometimes have to ask awkward questions. If I wasn't willing to listen to the answers, I wouldn't bother interviewing them in the first place.

HR Manager, retail company

17

DEALING WITH TRICKY QUESTIONS
WHAT TO SAY WHEN THERE'S NO CLEAR ANSWER

There are some questions that are not so much difficult as simply perplexing; tricky questions that don't seem to have a clear answer. How do you answer questions about your weaknesses, for example? How do you respond to questions about salary without doing yourself a disservice?

In this chapter we'll look at how to deal with these questions, as well as what to do when the interviewer seems to be inviting you to be critical or negative, and we'll see how questions like these can offer you a golden opportunity to demonstrate your integrity, intelligence and positivity. We'll also consider how to respond to those questions that seem to need only a yes or no answer. Do they really – or is there more to it than meets the eye?

Dealing with critical or negative questions

It's important that you remain positive and upbeat during your interview, showing interest and enthusiasm throughout. So what do you do when the interviewer asks you a question that seems to invite a negative answer? This section looks at how you can deal with these questions without criticizing your job and other people or criticizing yourself.

Invitations to criticize your job and other people

Sometimes interviewers seem to want you to be negative about your job or people you've worked with, asking questions like:

'What do you dislike about your current job?'

'What did you dislike about your last boss?'

'What are the sorts of things colleagues do that really irritate you?'

They're not actually interested in what you disliked; what they really want to know is if you're going to be a moaner or complainer. Are you going to criticize the company outside work? Don't take the bait. Smile, and give a neutral answer. This is the one time you *don't* give examples or anecdotes.

Example

Q *'What do you dislike about your current job?'*

Q *'What appeals to you least about this job?'*

'I find that [a routine task that everyone dislikes, such as filing or record keeping] is probably the least demanding part of my work. However, it's one of my responsibilities and important to the job as a whole, so I get it done as quickly and efficiently as I can, which allows me to attend to the more rewarding aspects of the job.'

Note how this answer also demonstrates your positivity and your competence.

Example

Q *'What do you think your last boss could have done better?'*

Q *'What did you dislike about your boss/supervisor?'*

'I always found X a very good employer/supervisor. I believe he/she gave me the best guidance possible and the opportunity to develop my career to the point where I'm ready for the challenges this new job presents.'

Invitations to be negative about yourself

Another sort of negative question appears to invite you to criticize yourself:

'What is your greatest weakness?'

'What do you find most difficult to deal with in yourself?'

'What would you change about yourself if you could?'

As before, the interviewer isn't really concerned with your weaknesses as such; what they're more interested in is how you react to implied criticism, your integrity and your degree of self-awareness. All these factors are keys to how well you will take guidance, or how much trouble you will be to manage, in the future.

The problem is that you are caught between two difficulties. Either you give an answer that reveals damaging flaws in your character, or you claim, improbably, to know of no imperfections in yourself. How do you give an answer that steers a path between the two? Look on questions like this as the opportunity to demonstrate your integrity, adaptability and positivity. You could try one of the following:

a 'flaw' that isn't a flaw in this specific context;

a humorous flaw that most people would sympathize with;

a former flaw that you've overcome;

a flaw that will have no impact on the job you're applying for.

A 'flaw' that isn't a flaw in this specific context

Check your cultural fit with the company you are applying to. Is there something about the company structure or ethos that makes your weakness significantly less of a problem?

Example

Q 'What is your greatest weakness?'

'I need structure. I get so involved with projects it's sometimes hard for me to draw the line.'

You know the company has a strong supervisory structure so you can safely reveal this weakness while also demonstrating your engagement with projects.

'In my current job, I frequently have to work alone on projects. I don't mind, but I think I do even better when I have a team to bounce ideas off.'

You know the company *always* works in teams so you can admit to this weakness without it being a problem.

A humorous flaw that most people would sympathize with

Example

Q 'What do you find most difficult to deal with in yourself?'

'My passion for chocolate...'

'Still expecting to wake up and find I'm a millionaire/rock star/Booker prize winner.'

However, by giving this sort of answer you run the risk that the interviewer will smile indulgently, then come back at you with a question about your weaknesses *with regard to your working life*.

A flaw you've overcome

Example

Q 'What sort of things do you find difficult?'

'I would once have said speaking in public and giving presentations was a bit of a problem, but since I went on a course last year to improve my skills I find that it's no longer a challenge.'

Note that this answer also demonstrates your positivity, competence and adaptability – your ability to learn and grow to meet demand.

'I used to have difficulty keeping up with all the filing the job entails. I've learnt from bitter experience to do it first thing in the morning so that I'm free to concentrate on more demanding responsibilities.'

Note that this answer also demonstrates your competence.

A flaw that will have no impact on the job you're applying for

Make sure you know what skills and competencies are necessary for the job and pick something that is not significant.

Example

Q 'What would you change about yourself if you could?'

'I'm not as strong in/good at xyz as I would like to be, but [say how you deal with it or are planning to rectify it.'

'I'm not as confident about giving presentations [useful but non-essential skill] as I would like to be, but it is getting better as I become more practiced.'

For a real ace, you could even take it one step further and swap a non-essential skill for an essential one:

'I'm not as confident about giving presentations [non-essential skill] as I would like to be. I much prefer using my interpersonal skills in one-to-one situations where I can really concentrate on the client [essential skill].'

Slightly more difficult are those questions that ask you to criticize your performance at work. The best thing to do is to treat them as flaws or problems you've overcome.

Example:

Q 'What do you find most difficult about your current job?'

Q 'What do you think you will find most difficult about this job?'

'I would have said [a difficulty you used to have such as handling spreadsheets or giving presentations] was/might have been a bit of a problem, but since I went on a course last year to improve my skills [or other positive action you've taken] I find that it's no longer an issue.'

Example:

Q 'What's the biggest mistake you've ever made in your job?'

The interviewer is asking for an anecdote that exposes one of your weaknesses. Make it a flaw or problem you had in the past that you've learnt your lesson from, along with the steps you took to overcome it:

'When I first started work, I could never see the point of filing – it was so boring and took up so much time. One day, the managing director himself came in and asked for a particular report sheet. Of course I hadn't bothered to file it and it wasn't in the pile I thought it was in. So I had to go through everything, with the MD getting more and more impatient and me getting more and more embarrassed. I spent the next three lunch breaks getting my filing sorted out and I've never let it slip since. I never want to be that embarrassed again.'

Questions about salary

How do you deal with questions the interviewer may ask about the salary you currently earn or the sort of salary you expect from this new job?

'What sort of salary are you expecting?'

'What do you think you're worth?'

'What is your current salary?'

The problem is, if you name a figure, are you underselling yourself, or are you pricing yourself out of the market?

It's difficult to answer a blunt question evasively, but if you say what your current salary is you could be creating problems for yourself:

They could just make you an offer as close as possible to your current salary, when they might have been prepared to pay more.

If your salary is much lower than that of the job you're applying for, they might think you're trying to jump too far ahead and miss out a career stage.

They might wonder why you had to take a low-paid job in the first place.

The salary for the new job might not be that much more than your current one, in which case would you take the job if they offered it to you?

Your current salary might actually be more than they are offering, especially if you're moving sideways rather than up.

They might wonder why you seem prepared to move into a lower-paid job.

Ideally, you don't want to mention a figure before they do. It helps to do your homework and try to get at least a rough idea of what the job is worth:

Are there similar jobs advertised where the salary is mentioned?

Does the organization have a fixed pay scale?

Are there salary surveys for your profession you could refer to?

Are there perks that would add to the package as a whole?

Can you talk to someone in a similar job? (Don't ask people bluntly what *their* salary is, by the way. Just ask what someone like *you* might be expected to get.)

Politely but firmly dodge any questions about salary until you are actually at the negotiating stage after they have offered you the job. Note that the offer of a job should not depend on the level of salary you are prepared to accept. The job should be offered first and the salary stated. It is up to you then to accept or reject the offer after negotiation.

Example

Q 'What is your current salary?'

'I think it would be misleading if I just gave you a simple figure. My salary is part of a much wider package that takes into consideration [include whatever else you currently receive – overtime pay, bonuses, perks, discounts, pension contributions, company car or staff facilities]. I could prepare an accurate figure if we needed to talk about it in more detail [when they offer you the job, for example].'

Example

Q 'We're offering around £22,000. How does that sound to you?'

'I believe current salaries for this type of job are around that figure, up to £27,000.'

You've done your homework, and you know roughly what the salary range is for the job. You are also aware that they are not saying 'The salary *is* £22,000'; they are just sounding you out. If you reply that it sounds fine, £22,000 is what you'll get, rather than the £25,000 they were prepared to go up to.

Example

Q 'What sort of salary are you expecting?'

Q 'What do you think you're worth?'

'I believe this sort of job attracts a salary of around £22,000 to £27,000. Bearing in mind my qualifications and experience, I would expect to be at the higher rather than the lower end of that range.'

As above, you've done your homework and can make an educated guess at the salary range.

Answering closed questions

An experienced interviewer should ask open questions that allow you to respond with full, example-laden answers. However, interviewers aren't always perfect and sometimes they ask closed questions which invite nothing more than a 'Yes' or 'No' answer. Some, of course, require nothing more than that, but you could be missing opportunities and selling yourself short if you answer all closed questions with a one-word reply.

Treat any closed questions as if they were open ones. Say 'Yes' or 'No' as appropriate, and then follow up with a relevant example or anecdote. Demonstrate your likeability – being open and communicative, your willingness to meet the interviewer more than halfway; and your adaptability – not being thrown by adverse circumstances.

Example

Open questions:

> *'What do you like about your current job?'*
> *'How do you get on with your colleagues?'*
> *'What would you say are the key skills for a manager?'*

Closed questions:

> *'Do you like your current job?'*
> *'Do you get on with your colleagues?'*
> *'Is leadership a key skill for a manager?'*

Example

Q 'Do you think attention to detail is important in this sort of job?'

'I would say attention to detail was very important in this type of job. If I may give an example, in my last position [say how checking details was part of the job and, how your eye for detail saved time, inconvenience or money for your employer].'

Note how the answer is softened very slightly by saying 'If I may give an example...'

Example

Q 'Do you like your current job?'

'Yes, I do like my current job. I particularly like [mention something relevant to the new job] and I can use my [skills and abilities relevant to the new job]. However, I believe that the position you are offering would allow me to [use or develop skills and abilities not currently fully employed].'

Here, the applicant has anticipated that the follow-up question to *'Do you like your current job?'* is likely to be *'Then why do you want to leave it?'* Note that, even though they want to change their job, they are still positive about the current one. Interviews are not the place for negative comments, even about past jobs or employers.

Some questions are not just tricky, they can seem downright crazy. How do you deal with the sort of question that's purposely intended to stop you in your tracks? That's what we'll look at in the next chapter.

KEY TAKE-AWAYS FROM CHAPTER 17

Anticipating tricky questions and thinking about how you can answer them will increase your confidence at interviews.

It will help you to learn how to:

- Side-step getting drawn into negative answers.
- Avoid admitting damaging weaknesses, mistakes and failures.
- Forestall awkward questions about salary and conditions.
- Open up closed questions to your advantage.

WHAT THE EXPERT SAYS

I need to know if someone is going to be difficult to work with. We're a small, high-precision company. Recruiting someone costs time and money that could be used elsewhere and employing the wrong person causes all sorts of problems with the rest of the staff. It could be a disaster.

Managing Director, engineering company

18

ANSWERING OFF-THE-WALL QUESTIONS
WHAT IS THE INTERVIEWER REALLY ASKING?

It's just possible that the interviewer will ask you a question that seems deliberately designed to throw you. Questions like:

How many cars would it take to completely block the M25?

If you were a vegetable, what type would you be?

What's wrong with the human body and how would you redesign it?

Who would you invite to a dinner party if you could have anybody?

How many cats are there in Aberdeen?

How would you re-invent the wheel?

Faced with a question like any of these, what on earth do you say? Is there even a right answer, and how would you be expected to know it if there was?

Although these questions are often more common in myth than in actual interviews, they do go through phases – going in and out of fashion – and could, unfortunately, be enjoying a period of popularity just when you're going through the job-hunting process. In this chapter you'll see that, however intimidating they appear, there is nothing to fear about these types of questions. Knowing how to set about answering them means you can tackle them coolly and calmly if and when they are thrown at you. You'll also be able to see them as an opportunity to demonstrate your intelligence, positivity and, especially, your adaptability – calm and poised whatever happens.

No interviewer asks a question for no reason, so what is the purpose of these seemingly crazy questions?

Off-the-wall questions originated in university interviews in an attempt to sort the wheat from the chaff in a situation where every applicant is more or less equally qualified in the same areas. They were an attempt to discover which interviewees could think on their feet with flair and originality under pressure, who could use their existing knowledge in novel and unexpected situations, and who would be prepared to extend their thinking skills outside what they comfortably knew and understood. They were designed to dig beneath the surface to find out what was going on inside the applicant's mind and establish what they might potentially achieve rather than what they had already accomplished.

Employers, especially in the newly established IT companies of the time, were quick to adopt the questions as one way of predicting interviewees' future performance where an established track record in such a new industry was rare. They subsequently became popular with creative and typically 'hi-tech' organizations and are now most often used by creative, blue-sky and leading-edge companies whether they are in media, technology, PR, retail or any other line of business.

So how do you answer them?

If you look at the examples above, you'll notice that there are actually two basic types of question:

Questions that ask you to work something out or estimate something you couldn't be expected to know offhand.

More 'psychological' questions asking you to define yourself, your likes and dislikes, or your personal attributes.

Each type of question has its own different approach which we'll look at in detail below. It's important to remember, though, that ALL questions, no matter how they're phrased, are about your suitability for the job. Bring every one of your answers back to that and you won't go far wrong.

Questions asking you to work something out

The point of these questions isn't about knowing the correct answer; you are deliberately being asked something you couldn't possibly know the answer to. Nor are they looking for some slick, 'clever' response. The question is genuine and the real point is to see how you go about working it out and whether you stay calm and unflustered while you do so.

Consequently, it's important to think aloud and show how your mind is analysing the problem. The temptation is to take a wild stab at the first answer that comes into your head. Resist it; it's not what's wanted. Instead, you need to explore, consider and evaluate. Gather any facts you do have and/or make educated guesses, giving your reasoning. Consider out loud what information you might need that you don't have and describe how you might go about getting it. Then outline how you would set about arriving at an estimate. Finally, round things off by giving some rough figures.

> **Example**
>
> *Q 'How many footballs would it take to fill the lift you came up here in?'*
> 'Let me think about that... The lift was about two metres high by two metres wide and deep, so the volume would be eight cubic metres. I'm not sure how big a football is without measuring but from memory I'd say it was about thirty centimetres. As a rough estimate you'd get three balls along a metre line, so... twenty-seven in a metre cube, and... two hundred and sixteen in an eight-metre cube, plus a bit more because three balls is ninety centimetres, not a full metre, so... very roughly, I'd say it was about two hundred and twenty footballs.'

Whether the lift was two metres wide or two and a half or one metre seventy, the exact size of the lift isn't the issue. What's important is that you were observant enough of your surroundings to make a guess and then think logically under pressure about the problem presented. It doesn't even matter that much about your mental arithmetic – through the ability to round numbers up or down to make calculation easy is a very useful one:

> '... twenty-seven in a metre cube, let's say thirty to make it easier... three eights are twenty-four, making two hundred and forty in an eight-metre cube, so... very roughly, I'd say it was about two hundred and twenty footballs.'

'Psychological' questions

These questions are designed to find out aspects of your character that aren't going to be readily apparent from your CV. They are especially popular with companies that have a clearly defined 'company culture' and/or a carefully nurtured brand identity and who need to be absolutely sure you will not only fit in with but actively contribute to that ethos.

Give the question proper consideration and be sincere in your answer. Don't just pick something at random; justify your choice and explain your reasoning. Remember, though, that they're not trying to delve into the deepest recesses of your psyche. They don't need your answers to reveal anything deeply meaningful about your psychology, just how you see yourself on a day-to-day level. They want to know what you're like to work with, so don't confuse what sort of person you are in private with what sort of employee you are.

Your research into the company will have given you a good idea of the company culture and an impression of the characteristics that they value, so match your answer to these. If this means giving an answer that is truly unrepresentative of you as a person, consider whether you would really be happy working there.

Example

Q 'If you were a fruit or vegetable, what sort would you be?'
What are your best, most relevant qualities for the job? What fruit or vegetable (or animal, or colour, or car, or whatever the question asks for) sums up those qualities? Your preparation for the interview should have included an assessment of your suitable characteristics, and if the interviewer had asked, 'What makes you a suitable person for this job?' you would be able to give a comprehensive answer. Treat it as essentially the same question:

> 'I think I would say I was an apple, because they are versatile – you can eat them raw or cook all sorts of dishes with them; they stand up well to knocks – unlike, say, peaches or strawberries; they get on well with most other fruits – you can add apple juice to sweeten any other sort; and, well, they're a good, honest, wholesome, dependable, down-to-earth sort of fruit.'

You may never face one of these off-the-wall interview questions, but if you do, understand that the interviewer is asking them for a reason, not just to wind you up. Take a deep breath, relax, and give yourself time to put together a reasonable response. Explain the logic behind your answer, and remember that all questions are ultimately about your suitability for the job.

So, now you can deal confidently with general questions, tricky questions, difficult questions and even off-the-wall questions. But what happens when it's your turn to interrogate the interviewer?

KEY TAKE-AWAYS FROM CHAPTER 18

This type of question is designed to see how you think, and whether you can think on your feet.

- Take your time, reason it out and do your thinking aloud - don't just make a blind stab at the answer.
- Keep the key qualities needed for the job in mind, especially when thinking through more 'psychological' questions.

WHAT THE EXPERT SAYS

Everyone here is employed for their unique creative abilities, there's no room for padding. I can't use someone who's just going to plod along in the same old tracks, so the point of the interview for me is to find out exactly who has got that break-out potential.

Creative Director, media company

19

YOUR QUESTIONS FOR THE INTERVIEWER

WHAT TO ASK AT THE END OF THE INTERVIEW

The interview isn't over yet. Having asked you everything that they want to know, the interviewer will ask if you have any questions for them. Your questions should convey your interest in the job and the company, so have some ready. No questions can look like you have no interest. Look on this as your best and last chance to demonstrate your intelligent curiosity, your positive motivation and to highlight your cultural fit.

Use the questions suggested in this chapter as a prompt, but try to think of the ones you really want answered. That's something that's going to be different for every job. The more appropriate and relevant the questions, the more it looks like you've done your homework on the position and the company, and the more interested and enthusiastic you look.

Two or three questions should be enough unless there are a lot of things you are genuinely unclear about. More than that, and the interviewer might worry about overrunning and keeping the next candidate waiting.

Try to avoid practical things that can wait until the job offer. Salary, hours and holiday entitlements can all be negotiated once the job is yours. For now, you're still being interviewed, so your task is to demonstrate how keen, intelligent and committed you are. Keep in mind that you are demonstrating your eagerness to make a contribution. Focus on what you can give and not on what you hope to get.

Areas you might want to ask questions about include:

The job itself – responsibilities, special projects, key goals, performance criteria. Don't ask the sort of thing you should be expected to know from reading the job specification, but you might want clarification.

Performance appraisal – appraisal schemes, review methods, pay and promotion reviews.

Company and/or department organization – whom you report to, who feeds into your department, where you fit in the organization.

Opportunities – travel, training, in-house schemes, qualifications, opportunities to branch out into extra responsibilities.

Career path – promotion opportunities, company expectations, company growth and development.

Here are some sample questions to start you thinking.

Q 'What are the main priorities of this job over the next six months?'
Q 'What are the biggest challenges facing the team/department currently?'

This question gets right to the core of the job and shows you as someone keen to take on and tackle key objectives. Even if the main tasks and responsibilities have been covered in the job description, try to find a way of phrasing the question so that you can find out from the interviewer what they consider the most pressing issues. It then gives you the opportunity briefly to recap any experience you've had dealing with similar situations or any specific skills you have that could be useful. It demonstrates that you are ready to take on responsibility and helps the interviewer to picture you doing so. It could also be useful information if they do offer you the job.

Q 'Why has the job become vacant?'

If this hasn't been answered already, it can be worth finding out why the last person left. If it's because they were promoted, you can then lead into a question about the company's promotion policy (see below). If it's a newly created post, you can ask about further company expansion (see below, again). If the present incumbent is moving on to better things after a long and happy career with the company, you can probably expect to do much the same yourself. If you get the feeling the interviewer is hedging and doesn't want to answer the question, you might want to probe a little deeper – 'Is there anything about their leaving I should be aware of?' Or you might just want to make a mental note to come back to the question should you be offered the job.

Q 'What would my career prospects be with the company?'
Q 'If I were to join the company, where do you see me in five years' time?'
Q 'Do you promote internally?'

It's nice to know what to expect. This question also suggests that, not only are you ambitious and intend to get on, but that you mean to stay with the company and let them benefit from your developing skills, knowledge, and maturity. You're not just showing commitment, but long-term commitment.

Q *'What are the company's current development plans?'*

Q *'How does the company see the job/department developing over the next few years?'*

This shows an interest in the company, demonstrates a sense of long-term commitment and also tells you what opportunities might arise in the future should you be offered the job.

Q *'I'm very interested in this job and I believe I could do it well. May I ask if you have any reservations about my suitability?'*

If you feel confident you can do it, this is a good question to ask. It lets you know almost immediately if you are being seriously considered at this stage. It also, of course, gives you the chance to recap your good points and reassure them about anything that they have doubts or are unclear about. You might even find they have genuinely overlooked or misunderstood something.

Q *'When can I expect to hear from you?'*

Q *'How will you inform me of your decision – letter, phone, e-mail?'*

For your own peace of mind, find out what the next stage in the process is, and when and how you will hear from them. Not asking makes you look as if you don't care.

KEY TAKE-AWAYS FROM CHAPTER 19

Your questions to the interviewer should reflect your suitability for the job as much as your interview answers do.

Base your questions on:

- The challenges and opportunities the job presents.
- Future developments for the job and the company.
- Career development plans and opportunities.

WHAT THE EXPERT SAYS

When the interviewer asks if you have any questions, don't ask about money or holidays; it doesn't make a good impression. I'm interested in people who are keen to develop, so questions about training and development opportunities are always good ones.

Helen Cole, Learning Services Coordinator, South West TUC

WHAT THE EXPERT SAYS

Ask about the job itself rather than terms and conditions. Show your interest and a sense of involvement. Interviewees can ask open questions as well as the interviewer; make it a two-way communication.

Janet Hembry, Head of Education and Skills Policy,
Government Office for the South West

20

VARIATIONS ON THE THEME

DIFFERENT TYPES OF INTERVIEW AND HOW TO DEAL WITH THEM CONFIDENTLY

As well as the straightforward one-to-one interview, there are a number of variations you might come across. These can be either instead of or in addition to the simple interviewer–interviewee set-up and can include:

screening interviews;

telephone interviews;

video interviews;

panel interviews;

serial interviews;

assessment centres;

informal interviews;

second interviews.

Screening interviews

As the name suggests, these interviews actually screen candidates out. They usually take place before the selection interview so that the interviewer doesn't have to interview anybody lacking the basic requirements. Cheaper, quicker and more immediate than an application form, and less effort than reading a CV, screening interviews ask a set of standard questions. If you get the answers right, you automatically go forward to a selection interview. If you get the answers wrong, you may still be able to apply again at a later date, and failure will not necessarily affect any future applications.

The interview rarely takes place face to face; usually it's on the phone or on screen. Questions can range from what your qualifications are to multiple-choice aptitude tests. The interviewer should explain before you start what is involved and how long it will take. If it isn't convenient, you weren't expecting it or you would like some time to prepare, explain politely and call back when you're ready. There's little you can do, though, to prepare for a screening test – the questions are usually fact based and you either have the basic requirements or you don't. There is no point arguing about the result, either, or asking if you can come in to discuss it; the person you're speaking to just doesn't have that authority.

Telephone interviews

It's very rare to have just a telephone interview; you usually have to undergo a formal face-to-face meeting as well. As above, these are mostly screening interviews to see if you meet the basic needs before being passed on to a selection interview. Other reasons why you might have an initial telephone interview are:

- because the job is phone based – customer enquiries or telephone sales, for example – and you are demonstrating an important skill required for the post;
- because it's a supposedly informal chat (see below for more about informal interviews) designed to find out more about you and see if you could be suitable for the job;
- because the employer is in a hurry to fill the post and needs to get up a shortlist quickly.

In all these cases, don't ring until you have the time, concentration and freedom from interruption to give a decent performance. It's a pre-interview interview, so make sure you have all the information you need to hand and are fully briefed and prepared. Have with you:

your CV;

your application letter or form;

the job advertisement, job description and any other information that will be useful;

your diary;

something to make notes on.

If they are calling you, ideally they will first send an email outlining when the call will happen, who will be interviewing you and brief details about what you can expect.

If they call you unexpectedly, stay calm. Remember to make a note of who's calling – name, position and company – and their phone number if it's going to be different from the one they are calling on. If possible, get hold of your CV and other useful information. Keep it to hand for just this sort of eventuality. If you're on a mobile and it's really not an appropriate place to take such an important call, tell them and ask if you can ring them back in a few minutes. Get to the best place you can at short notice – somewhere relatively quiet and calm – before calling back. The same applies if you are in an area with a poor signal.

While you are looking for a job and could be called by an interested company at any time, always check who's calling before you answer so that you can do so professionally and with poise.

When you're on the phone:

- *Speak clearly* – don't drink, chew or smoke while you're talking or even while the other person is talking. Be professional.
- *Smile* – it alters the muscles in your face and throat and makes your voice sound warmer and more relaxed. You can demonstrate your likeability even over the phone.
- *Make notes* – they could be useful for the formal interview, which would also demonstrate your competence.
- *Avoid one-word answers* – however unprepared you are, try to say more than just 'Yes' or 'No' in answer to questions. Show that you are adaptable, unflappable and prepared to engage with them.
- *Don't worry* – the person calling you won't expect you to be fully prepared or make the sort of presentation you would at a formal interview, but do make sure you sound enthusiastic and positive.

Video interviews

A cross between a telephone interview and a face-to-face interview, video interviewing via the internet, like video conferencing, is becoming increasingly popular.

When a company wants to interview you by video, they will email you the joining instructions before the meeting. Depending on the method they choose, you may have to download a specific app – just follow the instructions which will be fairly straightforward.

On the day, make sure that everything is working properly – including your internet connection – and fully charged. Treat the actual interview just the same as a face-to-face meeting but keep in mind some of the shortcomings of webcam images:

Prepare as fully as you would for any other interview.

Dress smartly, even if you are doing it from home.

Clear away foreground clutter that might intrude into the shot and distract the interviewer.

Be aware of what might be visible in the background, too.

If possible, keep a separate window open on screen that shows you what you look like so you can make sure you're in frame and looking into the camera.

Beware of patterns and stripes on clothing – they can produce interference patterns on screen that can be distracting.

If you are at home, make sure that you won't be disturbed.

Be aware that there is usually a slight time lag between broadcasting and receiving signals. Don't jump in to fill what seem to be gaps in the conversation.

Image and sound are not always perfect, so speak a little more slowly and clearly than normal – you don't need to take it to extremes.

Similarly, keep hand gestures and other movements to a minimum – waving your hands around will look odd on screen.

Remember to smile, just like you would in a face-to-face interview, and make appropriate 'eye contact' by looking into the camera lens.

Panel interviews

These are usually formal selection interviews where several people in turn ask you the usual questions, instead of just one. Where the hiring decision affects several people they can all be included on the interview panel. They typically include:

human resources manager;

technical manager;

department head;

line manager.

You will usually be told beforehand if it's a panel interview. Each member of the panel will have their own questions that address their particular concerns, so don't be unnerved by the thought that they're all going to question you. There probably won't actually be many more questions than there would be at a one-to-one interview. There is usually one person leading the panel who will take charge of the interview, welcome you and introduce you to the others.

The formalities of a panel interview can be a little tricky. Do you shake hands with everyone? Whom do you look at when answering the question?

On the whole, be alert to the situation and be led by the panel itself. If, for example, the leader stands up, shakes your hand and then asks you to take a seat, assume you don't shake hands with everyone else.

Make eye contact and smile as you are introduced to each member.

Try to remember their names and what their particular specialities are.

Always look at the person asking you a question.

When you answer, direct your answer chiefly to your questioner, but include the rest of the panel by glancing round and making eye contact.

Address your own questions to the panel leader, unless it's something clearly more suitable for the technical manager, for example.

At the end of the interview, thank the group as a whole for inviting you. Say how much you enjoyed it, that you found it interesting and that you look forward to hearing from them. Look around, smile and make eye contact as you do so.

Once outside, make a note of everybody's name and job title before you forget.

Serial interviews

Also called a sequential interview, this is similar to a panel interview, except that you have a one-to-one interview with each person in turn instead of all at once. Each interviewer is focusing on their own particular interest, and will ask you questions with a different emphasis. This means that overall you will undergo a very thorough investigation. Keep in mind what each person's concern is likely to be when you answer their questions. For example, though not exclusively:

human resources manager – career pattern and background, work style, training and qualifications, general educational background, training and development needs, salary and benefits;

technical manager – technical experience, specific knowledge, training and qualifications, technical skills, specific job-related problem solving;

department head or senior executive – cultural fit, ability to meet targets, contribution to profitability and growth, career aspirations;

line manager – working style, manageability, team fit, transferable skills, strengths and weaknesses, understanding of the job and ability to perform it.

The point of the serial interview is to get individual, unbiased assessments of you from each interviewer. This means you can start afresh with each person you meet. Even if you feel you failed to make a stunning impression on one interviewer, you have a couple more chances to claw back the situation. After the interview, the interviewers will get together to compare notes and arrive at a consensus decision that satisfies all parties.

Assessment centres

An assessment centre isn't so much a place as a battery of tests used to select employees. The technique was developed to select army officers during the Second World War when there was no time for leaders to emerge naturally and work their way up through the ranks. They use a range of assessment techniques overseen by trained and qualified observers. Several candidates are observed together working in a group, and discussion and teamwork are expected. Assessment tests can include:

interviews;

tests;

individual exercises;

group exercises;

indoor and outdoor tasks;

informal and social observation.

See Chapter 20 for some ideas for dealing with these sorts of tests and exercises.

Assessment centres for different companies follow their own individual programmes, lasting from half a day to two days and involving from five to 30 people at a time. Some are residential and nearly all involve some social interaction such as coffee, lunch or an evening meal. A typical programme might be:

DAY ONE:

Morning

Induction – meeting fellow candidates and assessors; introduction to the
    programme

Ice-breaker exercise

Aptitude and personality tests

Afternoon

Group problem-solving activity

Individual interviews

Evening
Group role-play exercise

DAY TWO:
Morning
Group case-discussion exercise
Individual in-tray exercise
Afternoon
Individual presentations
Individual interviews
Conclusion – question-and-answer session; next steps and leave taking

Prepare yourself fully for the interviews just as you would in any other situation. Do your research on the organization, understand the competencies they are looking for and know where, when and how you have demonstrated them. Don't forget, you are still under observation during breaks and meals – be on your best social behaviour.

Informal interviews

There is no such thing as an informal interview. Beware of the offer to 'get together for an informal chat'; it is never an occasion to relax and let your hair down even if it takes place in a bar or over a meal. An interview is an interview. If the person you are talking to has a job to offer, they will be weighing you up very carefully to see if you fit the role, so prepare as thoroughly as you would for any other interview. Let your interviewer take the lead and set the tone of the meeting. Follow their example as to the degree of formality or informality – using first names, for example. Use your social skills and be friendly and pleasant but don't drop your guard and be drawn into discussing anything or relating anecdotes that you wouldn't at a formal interview.

Second interviews

If you're invited back for a second interview, the company is seriously interested in you. Part of your task is to show that you are seriously interested in them, too. Find out more about them and the job, and prepare some intelligent questions about both.

It's a chance for them to find out more about you. That could mean a formal interview by a senior executive about your experience, skills and achievements, or it could be an 'informal' meeting over lunch to see how you get on with your potential colleagues. Remember: there is no such thing as an informal interview. You'll usually be told beforehand what to expect so that you can prepare for it. You'll also be told if the interview involves tests or exercises, presentations, or if you need to take examples of your work or projects you've worked on. If there was anything they seemed unhappy about at the first interview, expect to be closely questioned about it this time and prepare for that. However, if they weren't ready to be reassured they wouldn't have bothered to ask you to a second interview, so be positive.

KEY TAKE-AWAYS FROM CHAPTER 20

- Interviews can sometimes look different from the standard one-to-one across a desk.
- If possible, try to find out beforehand what the interview will consist of.
- Whatever form the interview takes, the key questions are still exactly the same – can you do the job? Will you do the job?

WHAT THE EXPERT SAYS

We're not giving you tests and things just to make you jump through hoops. We're genuinely trying to be fair. Why should someone who has genuine potential be overlooked just because they don't have good interview skills? Assessment has made us look more closely at people we might have ignored in the past, with very positive results.

HR Manager, engineering company

21

THE INTERVIEW: FUTURE TRENDS

TASKS AND TESTS THAT ARE ALREADY IN USE AND HOW TO PREPARE FOR THEM

The interview – future trends

Tasks and tests that are already in use and how to prepare for them

It's possible that within the next decade or so the one-to-one interview where you are simply asked a series of questions will become a rarity. More and more companies feel the need to see an applicant's actual performance in order to pick someone with the best fit for the job. Companies are becoming more inclined to 'audition' applicants rather that simply interview them – having the applicant come in for a pre-arranged period of time to demonstrate how they go about completing a set series of tasks relevant to the job, simulating real workplace activities.

For example, a sales person could be given a short briefing on a product then asked to make sales, either face to face or on the phone. A web designer could be given a client brief and asked to design a home page for them. You could be e-mailed a workplace problem with supporting documents before the interview and asked to deliver a report on it at a simulated departmental meeting with actual co-workers and managers.

Many of these tasks and tests already exist and are currently used during the selection process in some organizations, but they are likely to become much more widespread as companies become more focused on finding alternative, reliable ways in which your skills, qualities and specific suitability for the post can be assessed. Although there is no way to rehearse some of them, be as prepared as possible. You should be told when you're invited to the interview about any tests or presentations you'll be expected to go through, but you might like to check to make sure. Suddenly being faced with an unexpected aptitude test can throw even the most confident candidate.

Currently, these extras can take place before, during or after the rest of the interview, or they can be held on a different day altogether. They can include:

making a presentation;

showing your portfolio;

technical and attainment tests;

physical tests;

job-replica exercises;

role-play;

group exercises;

psychometric tests.

Making a presentation

You might be asked to make a short, formal presentation – either to the person interviewing you or to a panel or group of people involved in the hiring decision. What they are looking at is your ability to:

stand in front of a group and speak confidently;

arrange information coherently so that others can understand it;

explain key points clearly;

be concise;

think on your feet and respond flexibly to circumstances.

You'll be told beforehand what the presentation will be about and how long you'll have to deliver it. Always assume you will be asked questions afterwards and prepare accordingly even if it's not mentioned specifically. The sort of things you could be asked to do include giving:

a five-minute talk presenting your key qualifications for the role;

a five-minute outline of how you would develop the position given a free hand;

a 10-minute presentation on what you see as the three main priorities for the job;

a 10-minute profile of the key issues currently facing the industry;

a 10-minute presentation on why you believe you are suitable for the job;

a 15-minute analysis of the strengths, weaknesses, opportunities and threats facing the organization.

Plan and rehearse your presentation thoroughly before the interview, and don't forget to check what equipment will be available to you on the day. It's a good idea to make a summary of your presentation, preferably on one sheet of A4 paper. You can not only use it as a prompt yourself, but give it to members of the group as a handout. Plan thoroughly. It's always better to make a few points strongly and clearly than to cram too much in and confuse everybody. Don't run over time, either. If they say five minutes, they mean five minutes. Some companies are ruthless about cutting you off once your time is up and it would be a shame for them not to hear your final point, especially if you saved the best for last.

Showing your portfolio

In creative jobs especially, you can be asked to bring along a portfolio of your work. Don't leave it until the last moment to choose what to take. Pick things that have relevance to the job you're applying for, that you can talk about and that allow you to bring in some valid points and anecdotes. Showing your portfolio can almost be a mini-presentation. Rehearse it beforehand so that you can do it confidently and gracefully. Even if your 'portfolio' is a DVD, CD, PowerPoint presentation or website, you can still polish and edit it for the interview, practise introducing it, and prepare to answer questions about it afterwards.

If you are asked to leave work with a company or drop work in for someone to look at, be a bit wary. If possible, say that you would prefer to bring it in personally so you can discuss it and answer any questions they might have. If that's not possible, give them copies and avoid leaving originals or your one and only copy. Examples of your work are among your most valuable assets. Any loss or damage could hinder your prospects, and accidents do happen, unfortunately, especially to things lying around in offices.

Technical and attainment tests

You may be asked to give a practical demonstration of a skill essential for the job, such as driving, typing, translating and interpreting, or technical skills. Practise beforehand so that you're confident you can give a good performance under pressure on the day.

Physical tests

There are occasionally specific physical requirements for a job and you may be asked to take, for example, a sight test or hearing acuity test, or be tested for manual dexterity, colour blindness, etc. These tests cannot be done without your consent, but you are unlikely to be offered the job unless the tests are completed. It's possible you may also be asked to undergo a general health check for some jobs or by some organizations.

Job-replica exercises

These are practical demonstrations designed to assess how you'll behave in the job. They include things like:

in-tray exercises;

case studies;

role-play.

In-tray exercises

You're given a typical in-tray for the sort of job you want to do, including letters, phone messages, memos, reports, etc. You can also be interrupted by phone calls and e-mails while you work. Your task is to sort through it all and say or mark down how you would deal with each document or letter and what action, if any, you would take. It's designed to assess your management and organiza- tion skills as well as your ability to handle pressure and make decisions. One useful tip is to sort everything into three piles first:

urgent;

important but not urgent;

neither urgent nor important.

You can then work through the piles in order of priority. Read up on time- management and prioritization techniques to improve your confidence, and practise on your own in-tray.

Case studies

You may be asked to write a report or give a short presentation based on a brief- ing or case history about a relevant business matter. You have to assess the information and reach a decision, outlining your approach and reasoning. Brush up your familiarity with decision-making processes if necessary so that you feel confident you can handle the exercise under pressure.

Role-play

You could be asked to role-play a common workplace situation that you'd be expected to handle in the job. If you're told to expect a role-play exercise, think about the job, read the job description and try to anticipate what sort of thing you'll be asked to do. If the job is in retail, for example, it would be reasonable to expect a role-play dealing with customers – a difficult customer or a customer complaint, perhaps. For a management job, you could be asked to deal with a staff problem. The interviewer wants to see how, and how well, you deal not only with the problem, but also with the people involved and the stress of the situation. Stay calm, approach it professionally, and think about the sort of skills the interviewer is looking for.

In all cases the rules and expectations of any exercise should be explained to you clearly before you begin. If you have any doubts or aren't sure about anything, tell the person overseeing the exercise. Tell them, too, if there is anything that would make the test unnecessarily difficult for you – not having the right glasses with you, for example.

Group exercises

If teamwork is a major factor in the job, you could be asked to take part in a group exercise. These tests can last for anything from a couple of hours to a couple of days. They generally involve you interacting with a group to achieve some goal. What the goal is doesn't matter as much as how you work together as a team to achieve it.

The exercise should be assessed by trained observers who are scrutinizing things such as your:

contribution to the success of the team;

communication and interpersonal skills;

natural role within the team;

persuasion and negotiation skills;

judgement and reasoning;

problem-solving skills.

Your main tasks are to participate fully in the exercise and be a good team member. It doesn't matter so much whether you win or lose, but it really does matter how you play the game:

Avoid extremes. Don't take over and boss everyone around, but don't be too reserved, either, or opt out for any reason.

Avoid conflict. Give reasoned opinions when necessary but don't let them degenerate into arguments.

Take responsibility for seeing that everything in the team goes well:

Include members who seem to be on the fringes.

Find common ground when there is disagreement.

Summarize discussions and agreements so that everybody knows where they are, what they're doing and what the next step is.

Remind the group what their goal is and keep them focused on it.

Psychometric tests

The interview extras you are increasingly likely to encounter are the psychometric tests designed to give the interviewer an independent, unbiased view of your talents, characteristics and abilities. Psychometric tests fall into roughly three different types:

Aptitude tests. These measure your natural abilities and test for specific job-related skills such as verbal or numerical ability; spatial, mechanical or clerical aptitude; or logical thinking or reasoning skills.

Personality tests. These assess what sort of person you are and whether you have the personal qualities and characteristics thought right for a particular job. They usually ask what you would do or how you would feel in particular situations, or whether you agree or disagree with a given statement such as 'I enjoy meeting people' or 'I sometimes start things I don't finish.' The results are matched against an existing profile to see how well you fit.

Motivational and career interest tests. These are less common in recruitment; aptitude and personality tests are more popular. Motivational tests focus on what motivates and drives you, what you like doing, what stimulates you, where your natural tastes and inclinations lie, which occupations suit you best and so on.

What they have in common is that they are all 'paper-and-pencil' tests – though these days they're often taken on screen – devised by occupational psychologists, that ask you to answer multiple-choice questions rather than give a practical demonstration of a skill.

You'll usually be told when you get invited to the interview whether you'll be facing any psychometric tests. If it's not clear, find out:

whether there will be any tests;

what the aim of the test is: to explore your aptitude or to learn about your personal characteristics, or a combination of the two;

whether they can provide you with examples before the interview;

whether they know what sort of tests there are going to be – a Myers–Briggs personality test, a spatial reasoning or spatial recognition test, etc – so you can look them up and get an idea of what to expect;

how the tests will be taken – on screen, online or using paper and pencil;

whether you can use a calculator for numerical tests;

whether you will get feedback about the result;

when the tests will be taken – before or after the interview.

Knowing when you will take the tests can give you some idea of how important they are to the final decision. If you take them before the interview itself, it's possible they could be used for screening, and the decision will rely heavily on your having the right combination of abilities and characteristics, backed up by your performance at the interview. If you take them after the interview, it's more likely that the interviewer will make the initial decision, using the tests simply to confirm their own impression of you.

There is nothing to be scared of about psychometric tests, as long as you're prepared for them and ready to apply a little common sense.

Aptitude tests

Aptitude tests shouldn't require specialist knowledge or training, nor should they depend on your general knowledge. They are designed to measure specific natural inherent skills such as:

your ability to understand and work with numbers – useful in jobs where numeracy or the ability to handle data is essential;

your ability to use logic to solve problems – widely used to predict your general intelligence and ability to work your way through challenges;

your ability to understand and use words – valuable in jobs where you have to understand written instructions such as manuals, follow verbal instructions, assess information, or prepare information for others;

your ability to visualize in two and three dimensions – mainly used in jobs such as engineering, design and production, surveying and architecture, etc, where a grasp of how things fit together is essential;

your ability to understand and interpret diagrams – an advantage in jobs where the use of diagrams is common, such as engineering, computing, electrical, design and technical jobs;

your understanding of basic mechanical principles – used principally in jobs that entail assembling, running or maintaining machinery.

Only tests that are relevant to the job in question are chosen, and they give a precise score that allows the interviewer to see exactly what your aptitude for that particular skill is. Qualifying scores are set at a reasonable level – you simply have to be able to do the job competently, not be a genius.

Aptitude tests are usually in the form of puzzles where you're asked to do things like select the next number in a sequence, fill in a missing word, say whether a statement is true or false, pick out the missing diagram, and so on. The test is often timed but there's usually a chance for a short rehearsal first, answering a few specimen questions so you can get the hang of it and the tester can make sure you've got the right idea. Here are some examples.

Numerical question

Underline the next number in the sequence

1   5   9   13   17

Answer: (a) 21; (b) 23; (c) 19

Verbal reasoning question

Which is the odd one out?

(a) happy   (b) cheerful   (c) jovial   (d) precise

Abstract reasoning question

O is to o as OO is to:

(a) OOO; (b) oo; (c) Oo

Answers: (a), (d), (b).

Before you start the test, find out:

Whether the test is timed and, if so, how long you'll have to complete it.

Whether the test is negatively marked – meaning that you will actually lose points for wrong answers. This is unusual, but it can happen and will make a difference as to whether you should guess at answers you don't know.

Whether the questions will get more difficult as you go through them.

Whether you can have a practice run before the actual test to make sure you're doing it correctly.

Whether you can use any aids – a calculator for numerical questions, for example.

Although it's difficult to increase your natural aptitude for something without giving it years of practice, there are some useful points for doing aptitude tests that can help you improve your chances and get the best score you are capable of. They include the following:

Practise beforehand if you can. Familiarity will not only increase your confidence, it will help you work more quickly because you'll recognize what the questions are about. It will also alert you to some of the twists and turns questions can take (asking for the next *but one* in a sequence, for example).

Keep going. If you can't answer a question quickly, skip it and come back if there's time at the end.

If you really don't know the answer, make a guess – you have a one in four chance (for example) of being right. Make sure first, though, that you will not have points deducted for wrong answers.

When making a guess, first eliminate any answer that's definitely wrong, then make your choice from what's left.

With numerical questions, you can often avoid careless mistakes by roughly estimating the answer first. Is it likely to be in the tens or the hundreds? Where will the decimal point be? – and so on. This can stop you choosing a similar but wrong answer – 4.54 instead of 45.4, for example.

The questions in aptitude tests often get harder as they go on – ask about that before you start. When you feel you've reached your limit, go back, double-check your existing answers and fill in gaps rather than plough fruitlessly on. If you still have time after that, carry on with the difficult questions until asked to stop.

There are plenty of books and internet sites available that will allow you to run through sample tests. Look them up if you want to see what to expect and get some practice to improve your speed and confidence.

Personality tests

Different jobs suit different personalities. Some require you to be outgoing and involved with people; others need you to be self-reliant and able to work alone. Some jobs require you to analyse facts; others need you to assess feelings and instincts. Increasingly, employers believe that when they pick someone with the right sort of personality for a job, they will be better at it, progress more rapidly, be more enthusiastic about it, be more tolerant of the problems and setbacks associated with it, and be generally happier and more productive. Consequently, many now use personality profiling as part of the employee selection process.

Unlike aptitude tests, there are no right or wrong answers as such in a personality test, and the test is not usually timed. It's designed to predict how you will behave and relate to other people at work and usually involves multiple-choice questions, or questions that ask you to agree or disagree with a statement or to rank various statements in order of preference. These are easy if you have strong preferences, but more difficult if you like or dislike all the options more or less equally.

Example 1
Would you prefer to:

(a) present a lecture to a group of people?
(b) put together an engine from a kit of parts?

Example 2
I am interested in trying new things: YES   NO

Example 3
Friends often tell me their problems.
(strongly agree)   (agree)   (not sure)   (disagree)   (strongly disagree)

There are no right or wrong answers, and as you don't know exactly what profile is required for the job, there is little you can do to prepare specifically for a personality test. There are, however, some general points that can help you show yourself at your best:

Put yourself in a positive, professional frame of mind before you start. Think what you're like when you're at your best and base your answers on that. For example, a question asks if you enjoy meeting new people. Virtually everyone has had times when they would prefer to relax at home rather than have to go out and deal with strangers. The point is how you *usually* react, and how you expect to behave professionally, not what you do occasionally.

The better you know yourself, the easier it will be to answer the questions. Practise doing personality tests and questionnaires, so that you have a chance to think about your preferences, how you behave and how you react in everyday situations.

Think about the job. While it's difficult to skew the results of personality tests, most of us adopt roles for specific jobs and emphasize different sides of our natural personalities accordingly. Think about the role you need to play in the job you're applying for: will you need to wear your empathy hat or your efficiency hat, for example? Weigh your answers accordingly.

Don't overlook the obvious. If the job is in sales or customer services, for example, questions that ask whether you like being with people, get to know them easily, and enjoy social situations clearly need a positive answer.

Try to answer all the questions. The more you leave out, the harder it will be to form an impression of you. If in doubt, trust your gut instinct and go with the answer that first occurs to you.

Be honest, confident and up front about who and what you are. While it's possible to 'invent' the right personality profile for a job, it's virtually impossible to do so consistently throughout an entire questionnaire. You may be mistaken about what they want, anyway. What if you present yourself for a management job as a tough-minded, results-oriented go-getter, when they've decided the post needs a supportive, team-focused people person?

Online tests

Online tests are becoming increasingly popular. Their content is very much the same as that of any other sort of aptitude or personality test, the only difference being that you complete the test on screen rather than using a paper and pencil. They are sometimes used on company websites as a way of screening potential applicants before they even get to the interview stage.

The tests are not designed to check your keyboard skills, so the actual process should be straightforward. You should be provided with full instructions and the opportunity to practise a couple of questions. Complete the tests as you would any others, but make sure you are aware of a few things before you start:

Do you need to enter a code number or password before starting?

Does the format allow you to go back and answer questions you've missed out?

Can you change answers after you've entered them?

Will you get feedback and, if so, how?

To recap, the general tips for doing any form of psychometric test, whether an aptitude test or a personality test, on paper or on screen, are as follows:

Keep calm.

If you have any condition that might make the test more difficult for you – partial sightedness, dyslexia, or even not having your reading glasses – tell the person giving you the test and they can make suitable arrangements.

Read the instructions carefully all the way through.

Take full advantage of any practice questions you can do before the timed part of the test.

If there's anything you don't understand, ask the person giving you the test.

If you have any problems during the test – a broken pencil, missing page, disturbing noise outside or bright light in your eyes, for example – let the person administering the test know immediately.

Future possibilities

As we've said, tests are becoming increasingly popular as an objective means of assessing suitability, rather than relying on the interviewer's gut instinct alone. Employers see them as quick, reliable, impartial and fair, and are keen to add to and refine them. The sorts of tests that could well find their way into the interview process in the future include the following.

Emotional intelligence tests

These are personality tests that predict the likelihood of your success by analysing the possession of life skills such as:

self-awareness – the ability to understand and control your own feelings;

emotional resilience – the ability to adapt to situations and recover from setbacks;

motivation – drive, energy and enthusiasm;

interpersonal sensitivity – empathy and respect for others;

influence and persuasion – the ability to influence others positively;

intuitiveness – the ability to trust your instincts;

conscientiousness and integrity – honesty, commitment and reliability.

Cognitive process profiling

Another type of personality test, one that looks at how you think, how you approach problems and your preferred method of working. It can predict whether you will be more comfortable dealing with concrete tasks, parallel processing or strategic thinking when it comes to problem solving, among other things.

Virtual reality

Already widely used for selection and training in the navy and air force, simulated reality tests could become more widespread, testing your reaction rates, dexterity and ability to think on your feet and respond to emergencies in a variety of situations.

Business learning tests

One stage on from job-replica exercises, business learning tests teach you what you need to know in order to carry out a task and then assess your ability to apply that learning in specific situations. They require no previous knowledge, but they do test your ability to both take in and use information reliably, appropriately and intelligently.

KEY TAKE-AWAYS FROM CHAPTER 21

- Organizations are always looking for better ways to predict how you will perform in the actual job.
- Be aware of all the possibilities that could be included and understand how to deal with them.
- When you're invited for an interview, it's fine to ask if any tasks or tests will be included as part of the interview.
- Remember that they are tests, not tricks. The key questions are still exactly the same: can you do the job? Will you do the job?

WHAT THE EXPERT SAYS

Don't make things difficult for the interviewer. For example, we ask people to give a short presentation. We tell them it's 10 minutes, but some people still run over. What do you do? If you allow them 12 minutes, it puts the people who stuck to 10 minutes or under at a disadvantage. I let them run over but I resent it and it puts my back up for the rest of the interview.

Mark Riches, Unit Manager, Health Protection Agency

22

LOOKING THE PART
MAKING A GOOD IMPRESSION FROM THE START

You've done your research, got all your answers prepared and are ready for any question the interviewer might throw at you. All you need to do now is make sure you look the part.

You need to create the right impression from the very first moment of the interview. By the time you're sitting down answering questions, it may be too late. The interviewer will begin to form their opinion the second you step through the door, so make sure they get the right idea from the start. This chapter focuses on the positive impression you can make with your appearance and your body language – how you look and how you behave – and suggests ways you can put yourself across with confidence and assurance even when you feel nervous.

Your appearance and behaviour should convey the same message that your answers to the interviewer's questions do – that you are intelligent, friendly, adaptable, competent and positive, that you have integrity and that you can do the job. Everything about you should support this message, from the clothes you wear to the way you sit.

Appearance

Your general appearance

It hardly needs saying that when you go for an interview you must look clean, groomed and smart. Take a little extra care with your appearance, apply a little extra polish and the results will be worth it. Everything you've been told is true – interviewers do notice things like clean fingernails and nicely polished shoes, so pay attention to the details. Things like that help to make you feel confident about meeting strangers and being judged by them. More importantly, they show that you've made the extra effort. Nothing impresses interviewers more than someone who's made an effort.

How you dress

Look as if you belong. Dress like a smarter, more polished version of the staff already employed. The working environment is all about teamwork, so if you look like part of the team you're already ahead of the game.

- If you're applying for a job in a field you already know well and are a part of, this shouldn't pose too much of a problem. Lawyers and accountants nearly always dress like lawyers and accountants; design and media people dress like design and media people the world over.
- If you're entering a new industry you'll need to do some research to find out what the dress code is.
- Look at the photos on their website, company brochures, newsletters and other material to see what type of image they want to project, as it will help you avoid sticking out like a sore thumb.
- Shots of people all looking formal in suits and ties tell you that nothing less than a smart suit for both men and women will do for the interview.
- If, however, the home page features pictures of the staff in jeans and T-shirts, then smart casual wear will fit in better.
- If in doubt, ask someone who works in that type of job what they recommend, go and see what employees going in and out of the building are wearing, or simply ring the company, say you have an interview there and ask what the dress code is.

In general, you want to present a highly professional appearance in the manner most appropriate for your chosen field. Whether you're dressed in a three-piece suit or chinos, the way to look like a professional is:

Be clean, fresh, tidy and well pressed.

Dress for an important meeting or presentation rather than your average day.

Avoid extremes – if in doubt, lean towards a neutral style and colour.

Avoid fussy accessories – it's too tempting to fiddle with them when you're nervous.

Avoid anything jokey when choosing ties, earrings, bags or briefcases, etc – it will cancel your authority immediately.

Avoid anything too short or too tight, as this will also undermine your professionalism.

Dark colours convey professionalism better than light ones.

Plain colours are less distracting than busy patterns.

Quality shows. Well-cut clothes in natural fibres with a good finish are essential whether you're wearing a suit or business casual wear.

It's tempting to buy a new 'interview outfit' just for the big day. If you do, wear it at least a couple of times before the interview, even if only at home. Make sure that the outfit is comfortable and trouble free and that you can sit comfortably in it without anything riding up, twisting round or creasing, and that you can stand up and shake hands without anything gaping or straining. Having to adjust bits of clothing continually will distract both you and the interviewer.

Posture and bearing

Some people can wear the most expensive clothes and still give the impression they've just borrowed them for the occasion if they carry themselves badly. You have to convey the idea that you're keen and capable, and project your confidence and interest:

Think up and open – stand tall, head up, shoulders back.

Remember to breathe.

Aim to be alert and poised in your manner and gestures.

Avoid clutching bags or folders so hard your knuckles go white.

Look around you rather than at the floor – take in your surroundings.

Meet people's gaze and make eye contact.

Smile.

Behaviour

First impressions

Get off to a good start and not only will the interviewer be impressed, but you'll feel confident too. That confidence will help carry you through the first few questions until you relax and get into your stride. You look good; you're dressed well; now greet the interviewer in a friendly and confident manner:

Before you even enter the room, take a moment to centre yourself. Stand tall, pull your shoulders back and your head up. Take a slow, deep breath and let it go.

Smile as you enter.

Close the door behind you.

Make eye contact with the interviewer – and with anyone else in the room.

Be ready to shake hands when they introduce themselves.

Say 'Hello, very nice to meet you' or 'Pleased to meet you' or any other of the usual greetings.

Sit down when invited to.

If the interviewer forgets, wait for a moment before asking 'May I sit down?' or 'Is it OK if I take a seat?'

Be alert to the interviewer's behaviour and follow their lead. Let the interviewer take the initiative and be ready to respond appropriately.

This is the interviewer's territory, so don't attempt to dominate it – hence the advice to wait before shaking hands and sitting down so that the interviewer can take the lead and remain in control. It's not just politeness; it's essential psychology.

Keeping up the good work

Keep the right impression going throughout the interview. By now, your answers should be doing much of the work for you and all that careful preparation is starting to pay off. Underline your suitability with great body language. You want to come across as confident, enthusiastic, responsive and energetic, as well as interested, alert and intelligent. You also want to appear reliable, so develop a moderate voice, controlled gestures and a calm yet keen disposition:

Sit well back in your chair rather than perching nervously on the edge.

Sit upright with both your feet on the floor and your hands resting in your lap or on the arms of the chair.

This position should help you appear alert yet relaxed and help you to avoid nervous or defensive mannerisms such as folding your arms, crossing your legs, fidgeting, tapping your feet, biting your nails, etc.

Keep your head up and look at the interviewer with an interested expression – lean forward slightly in a listening position.

Let your gaze move around the interviewer's face – forehead, eyes and mouth – as you talk. This helps you maintain good eye contact while avoiding a fixed stare.

Nod intelligently while your interviewer explains things to you or asks you questions.

As you relax, allow your natural gestures to emphasize points and show more of your character.

If you feel yourself getting bogged down or lethargic, pull yourself upright, breathe in and concentrate on being up and open with your posture, gestures and facial expression. It should make you look and feel alert and energetic again.

If, on the other hand, you start to feel uncontrolled and nervous, glance away, breathe in deeply from your stomach, relax your shoulders and let your hands rest on your lap for a moment. You'll look like you're taking a moment to consider and you can resume your answer with renewed poise.

Remember to smile frequently throughout the interview.

Lasting impressions

Having established a good impression and maintained it throughout the interview, leave a good impression behind you when you go:

Be alert to 'winding up' signals from your interviewer.

They might say something like 'We'll be in touch early next week' and thank you for coming in to see them.

Make eye contact.

Smile.

Shake hands.

Thank them for seeing you.

Add something like 'It's been very nice meeting you; I look forward to hearing from you soon' or 'It's been a very interesting afternoon; I look forward to your decision.'

Leave; don't linger.

The interview isn't over until you're off the premises. Wait until then to loosen your tie, light a cigarette or whatever.

Overcoming nerves

Everyone dreads looking nervous in interviews, but, oddly enough, interviewers are quite tolerant. Believe it or not, they actually want you to do well and will usually try to help you display your best qualities. The interviewer has a vacancy to fill. If they don't, they've got a real problem. You could be exactly the person they need, so they're not going to rule you out just because you seem a bit jittery at the start. Only if nerves persist throughout the whole of the interview (they'll worry about your reactions to stress) or stop you giving coherent answers (they'll never find out what you can do) will they be a major problem.

Don't let fear of nerves prevent you from making a positive impression:

Thorough preparation of the sort outlined in this book will improve your confidence. You will understand what they want, why you are right for the job and how, where and when you have demonstrated that.

Practising interview skills – entering a room, shaking hands, etc – and rehearsing answers to interview questions will make them feel more familiar.

Getting organized before the interview will help you avoid unexpected setbacks:

- Make sure you know exactly where the interview is and how to get there.
- Double-check the date, time and name of the person you're meeting.
- Get everything ready the night before, including a copy of your CV or application form, name, address and phone number of the company, fully charged mobile in case of accidents or delays, car keys or money for fares, and any other documents or equipment you need for the interview.

Arrive at your destination a little early. When you get there, ask for the cloakroom and check your appearance thoroughly – hair, teeth, make-up, all your buttons and zips, and any runs or unravellings. Don't forget the obvious reason for using the cloakroom, either – nerves have a terribly stimulating effect on the bladder.

Avoid tea and coffee for an hour or so before the interview – caffeine can make you jittery and it, too, has a stimulating effect on the bladder. Alcohol is best avoided altogether.

Do this quick relaxation exercise to get your nerves under control. Try it a couple of times on the way to the interview and when you're checking your appearance in the cloakroom. It's very unobtrusive, so you can do it while you're waiting to be called as well:

Relax your shoulders and arms.

Breathe in slowly to the count of three.

Hold your breath for the count of three.

Breathe out slowly to the count of five.

Breathe in to the count of five.

Hold your breath for the count of five.

Breathe out to the count of seven.

Breathe normally.

If you start to feel nervous during the interview, remember that:

A deep breath will relax your chest and release tension.

A smile will help relax rigid face muscles.

Nodding slowly while the interviewer is speaking will release neck tension.

Nerves can make you physically close up – hunched shoulders, folded arms, crossed legs, lowered head. Take a moment every so often to open up consciously – head up, shoulders back, feet on the floor, hands on chair arms or on lap. Breathe in and answer the question.

You can also take your focus off your nerves by deliberately practising your like-ability skills. Concentrate on the interviewer and think about meeting them half-way, putting them at their ease and making it a good experience for them. Nothing has a more calming effect on stress than taking your mind off yourself and putting it on someone else.

KEY TAKE-AWAYS FROM CHAPTER 22

- Your appearance and behaviour should match the personal and professional qualities you want to display.
- An interview is a formal occasion and there are certain conventions associated with that.
- Don't let nerves rob you of the chance to shine – there are ways to overcome them.

WHAT THE EXPERT SAYS

First impressions count. I naturally prefer someone who's made an effort; it means they're interested enough in the position to want to make a good impression on me. I look for someone who is appropriately dressed, confident but not overconfident and with good body language. The first 10 seconds really are important – the greeting, the handshake. Get that wrong and you spend the rest of the interview trying to retrieve the situation.

Mike Tredrea, HR Manager, West Pharmaceutical Services

WHAT THE EXPERT SAYS

It's nice if someone is friendly and confident from the start – it means I can relax, too. I feel if someone is too self-conscious, it could mean they're more interested in themselves than they are in the job.

HR Manager, retail company

23

WHAT HAPPENS NEXT?
WHAT TO DO AFTER THE INTERVIEW

While you're waiting for their decision

Make notes

Immediately after the interview, while it's still fresh in your mind, write down some notes about:

who you saw – name and title;

any useful information they gave you about the job and the company;

how the interview went;

the sort of questions they asked;

what went well;

anything you would do differently next time;

what will happen next – if there will be a second interview, when they'll contact you, etc.

These notes will be useful for your records, and also when you go to your next interview – whether that's a second interview with the company, or with another employer. Recalling what questions they asked can be helpful. Were there unexpected areas of your skills and competencies that were focused on? Were there problems in your previous career or work record the interviewer picked up that you hadn't anticipated? Use the experience to polish and perfect your next performance.

Write a letter

After the interview, that day or the next, send a brief letter or e-mail thanking the person who interviewed you, or the leader of the panel if it was a panel interview. This serves several purposes:

It creates a good impression – it's polite, it looks thorough and it conveys enthusiasm.

It gives you a chance to recap your suitability for the job, your enthusiasm for it and the key benefit of employing you.

You can include anything important you missed out at the interview.

It puts your name and suitability at the forefront of the interviewer's mind.

The letter on the next page gives an example. This letter can also be adapted easily for e-mail, of course.

If they don't make you an offer

Bad luck. You were right for the job or they wouldn't have asked you to the interview. Unfortunately, it was someone else's turn to be picked. Look on the bright side, though: that successful candidate won't be at the next interview you go to.

There are several reasons why you might not have been selected this time:

The interviewer didn't believe you had the skills or experience necessary to do the job.

They weren't convinced you understood sufficiently what the job entailed or required.

They didn't think you had the personal qualities such as energy, stress-hardiness or ambition to be successful in the job.

They didn't feel you fitted in – with the team profile, the company culture or whatever.

Note that the reasons above focus specifically on what the interviewer thinks, feels or believes. They may be right or wrong. Their conclusion might be entirely factual, or based on their own misunderstandings and prejudices. They might, on the other hand, be entirely a result of your own failure to convince them. Your task next time is to be so convincing they can't overlook your suitability. Examine each of those areas carefully before the next interview and try to see where any flaws were. Make sure that:

You know from the job ad and the job description (and any other information you can get hold of) exactly what the job entails.

You have the skills and competencies required.

First line of your address
Second line of your address
Third line of your address
Postcode

Telephone number
E-mail address

Date

Name of interviewer
Position
Company name
Address line one
Address line two
Address line three

Dear [Mr, Mrs, Ms – Name]

Thank you for interviewing me for the post of [whatever you are being interviewed for] yesterday [include the date]. I greatly appreciated the opportunity to meet you and find out more about [the company or organization]. It was very interesting to see/hear about [something that impressed or interested you] and to see/hear/understand/experience [something else that stuck in your mind].

Having heard about the work in more detail, I believe I could make a significant contribution to [the company, organization, department, project]. My current experience in [what you do or the most relevant facet of it] has developed my [specific skill, area of experience or responsibility] and my [another relevant strength] to the high level required by your organization. I should also add that [now is the time to mention anything relevant you didn't get a chance to include in the interview].

May I confirm that I would be very interested in taking this position with your company. It offers the opportunity I am looking for to [develop my career, my skills, professional growth, experience, whatever fits your particular circumstances]. I would welcome the chance to work in/with [your team, for example] and believe [in time] I could contribute substantially to the success of [the company, department, project].

I hope you will consider me favourably. I look forward to hearing from you.

Yours sincerely

Your signed name

Your typed name

You can give examples of how, when and where you've demonstrated these in the past.

You can present these examples confidently and enthusiastically.

You display in your appearance and behaviour the personal qualities they want.

Keep in contact

If you really liked the look of the job and felt the company was a good place for you to work, don't give up at the first hurdle. It's worth keeping in contact with them because there's always a possibility that:

the successful candidate initially accepts the job, but their current employer offers them a better deal to stay on;

the successful candidate only stays in the job a couple of months – maybe they weren't right for the job or they found a better one after accepting, or maybe the job didn't turn out to be what they wanted;

another, similar job comes up in the same company.

Swallow your disappointment and reply to their rejection letter. By doing so, you maintain the good impression you worked so hard to establish and remind them that you are still interested in the job and the company. The letter on page 231 gives an example.

If you are still interested and haven't found anything better after three to six months or so, contact the person who interviewed you again – by letter or e-mail – to keep you and your interest fresh in their mind. An example of this kind of letter is shown on page 232.

Keep in contact for as long as you're still looking for the right opportunity to come up. Even if a suitable vacancy doesn't open there, your interviewer may hear of something in another department, branch or organization and let you know about it.

Keep applying

Get as much interview experience as you can. The more you do, the better you get, so that when your chance of a lifetime comes up you won't miss out because you are unprepared.

Don't wait for the result of one interview before applying for the next. You need to keep up the momentum. If you get a rejection, it's much easier to shrug and put it down to experience if you have another three or four promising meetings lined up and five or six applications in the post.

First line of your address
Second line of your address
Third line of your address
Postcode

Telephone number
E-mail address

Date

Name of interviewer
Position
Company name
Address line one
Address line two
Address line three

Dear [Mr, Mrs, Ms – Name]

Thank you for your letter of [the date]. Although I am naturally disappointed at not being chosen for the position of [whatever it was], I would like to thank you for taking the time to consider my application.

What I saw of the company at the interview interested me greatly, and I would still like the opportunity to work for you. I would, therefore, like to ask if you would keep my name and details on file for consideration should the situation change or another vacancy arise.

Yours sincerely

Your signed name

Your typed name

First line of your address
Second line of your address
Third line of your address
Postcode

Telephone number
Email address

Date

Name of interviewer
Position
Company name
Address line one
Address line two
Address line three

Dear [Mr, Mrs, Ms – Name]

You may remember interviewing me for the post of [whatever you were being interviewed for] on [the date of the interview]. Unfortunately, I was unsuccessful on that occasion, so I am writing to you again to see if any opportunities have arisen in the meantime. Although I was disappointed at not being chosen for the post, I was very interested in what I saw of the company at the interview and would still like the chance to work for you.

I am [remind them what you do] with a sound background in [remind them what your background is] and many/several/some years' experience of [your experience that would be of benefit to the company]. Since our last meeting, I have [tell them about any skills, qualifications or experience you've gained in the meantime].

I believe I have the skills and abilities that fit well with your need for first-rate staff [for example], and I believe I could make a valuable contribution to [the company, organization, department, team].

I look forward to hearing from you.

Yours sincerely

Your signed name

Your typed name

After every interview and before the next, look over your notes and review your performance. Is there anything you could do better next time? Is there any area you could strengthen or polish?

If they do make you an offer

Congratulations, they want you. You now have to decide if you:

want the job, no question;

want the job subject to negotiation;

might want the job if a better offer doesn't materialize;

don't want the job.

If your answer is no or maybe

If you don't want the job, tell them so immediately: they'll want to offer it to some-one else as soon as possible. Be polite, though; you may want to apply to them again in the future.

If you might want the job, contact them immediately, thanking them for their decision. Be enthusiastic and positive, but ask for a day or two to think it over. It's better to do it this way than simply avoid calling them until you've made a decision.

While thinking it over:

Weigh up the pros and cons of the job you're currently in, or your current situation if you're unemployed, and decide if you want to stay or go and at what price.

Weigh up the pros and cons of the job you've been offered and see if it's worth accepting regardless of whether it's the only one on offer or not.

Contact any potential employers who have interviewed you but not yet made an offer. Explain the situation and ask if they are in a position to make a decision. Even if they're not, they should at least let you know if you're definitely out of the running, which should make your choice easier.

If you have interviews to come or promising applications in the system, you have to make an educated guess about their likely outcome.

Weigh up the importance of the offer. Getting an offer on your first interview might be very different from finally getting one after a dozen or so interviews.

Negotiation

Having just been offered the job, you are in a very strong position to bargain. Unless they state categorically that the offer is standard for all employees at that grade and non-negotiable, ask for the best deal you can get. As long as you remain reasonable and polite, there is little chance you'll negotiate yourself out of the job. If they can't meet your requests, they'll just tell you they can't and put the ball back in your court. Accept it gracefully and either carry on bargaining or give in, depending on your skill and confidence as a negotiator.

- Before you start negotiating, decide if there are any deal breakers – a salary below which you won't go, hours you can't work and so on.

- Know your worth. Reread the job description and requirements. If you have more than they ask for – qualifications, experience, training, extra computer skills or a language, for example – and it's relevant to the job, that could be a useful tool.

- Get clued up about all the added extras available – what does the company offer other employees? What do other similar companies offer? Can you negotiate childcare contributions, car or travel allowance, expenses, a laptop, mobile phone or pocket PC and so on?

- Are you prepared to offer any concessions – cover extra duties in exchange for a higher salary, for example?

- Be prepared to compromise. If they can't offer a higher basic salary, are you willing to accept other benefits such as higher commission, increased overtime, bonuses, or the promise of a pay review in six months, for example, to make up the difference?

- Your working conditions might be negotiable as well – location, type of office, starting and finishing hours, for example.

Once you've finished negotiating and agreed a deal that you're both happy with, you should receive a formal offer letter along with your starting date. Make sure you know exactly what the job entails and what you are being offered in return before you formally and bindingly accept the offer in writing. Give your notice to your current employer only when you have everything in black and white, not before – accidents can always happen. Notify anyone else who might need to know, such as companies that have just interviewed you or are about to do so – don't just leave them in the lurch.

KEY TAKE-AWAYS FROM CHAPTER 23

- You can learn from every interview and use it to prepare for the next.
- Always take the opportunity to follow up an interview with an email or letter – it takes little effort compared to getting an interview in the first place.
- Try to have more than one iron in the fire at all times.
- If an offer isn't quite right, it's worth trying some polite negotiation to see if can be improved.

WHAT THE EXPERT SAYS

My decision to employ somebody is not necessarily based on their availability. If they're the right person, I'd rather wait three or four months while they work out their notice rather than lose them. I hope they're going to be with us for some years, so what are a few more months? I also hope they're going to be loyal, so why penalize them for showing loyalty to their previous employer?

Tina M Buchanan, Group HR Director, Hamworthy Combustion Engineering

24

INTERVIEWS IN A NUTSHELL

THE THREE ESSENTIAL QUESTIONS YOU NEED TO KNOW ABOUT

So many questions, so many answers. If, after reading through the rest of this book, you are still feeling confused and concerned that you are never going to remember everything, especially in the stressful situation of an interview, don't worry. This is where we organize all that information and put it into perspective.

Remember right back at the beginning when I said there are three things that employers want? All they want is:

- Someone who can do the job.
- Someone who *will* do the job.
- Someone who fits in.

This means there are, essentially, only three questions that the interviewer is really asking:

- Can you do the job?
- Will you do the job?
- Will you fit in?

All the questions asked at interviews are simply variations on these three themes.

Main Question 1: Can you do the job?

Have you got the skills and experience needed to perform the tasks required? Variations on this theme include questions such as:

- What does your current job entail?
- What experience do you have to do this job?
- Why do you think you are right for this job?
- What are your strengths?
- What can you bring to the job?
- What kinds of decisions do you have to make in your current job?
- What would you say makes a good… [*what your job is*]?
- How would you approach… [*a typical work problem*]?
- Tell me about a time when you… [*tackled a typical work situation*].
- What do you do when… [*a typical problem arises*]?

Know what skills and experience the job requires. Know what skills and experience you have. Think about how they are going to fit together in this new job. Consider broad skills such as being a good organizer or good at communicating as well as specific technical skills.

Main Question 2: Will you do the job?

Are you an enthusiastic, motivated individual with a good work ethic? Variations on this theme include questions such as:

- Why do you think this is the right job for you?
- How well do you work under pressure?
- What are your long-term career plans?
- What is your attitude to challenge?
- What are your greatest achievements?
- How do you define doing a good job?
- What are you looking for in a job?
- What motivates you in your job?
- What do you feel it takes to succeed in this field?
- Would you say you had ambition?

Know what the positive aspects of the job are. Know what positive qualities you have. Think about how you can bring these positive elements together. Consider how this job and this company fit into your overall career plans.

Main Question 3: Will you fit in?

Are you a willing team member who understands what we are trying to achieve and who will support and contribute to that? Variations on this theme include questions such as:

- Do you work well with others?
- What would you say makes a good team member?
- Do you get bored… [*doing a routine task*]?
- Describe a problem you had with a colleague (supervisor, customer) and how you overcame it.
- How do you react to criticism (advice, suggestions, instructions)?
- What would your colleagues say about you?
- What is your preferred way of working?
- How do you approach a project?
- What do you know about our company?
- How would you describe this company?
- What do think the key developments in this industry are going to be?

Know what the company's culture and values are and how they fit with your own personal style. Consider what makes a good employee and a good colleague and the personal qualities you have that help you to be both.

Get the answers to these three questions clear in your own mind, know your own worth and value and be sure about how you are going to present these answers to the interviewer, and you will sail through almost every interview you are ever likely to encounter.

All that's left to say is: good luck in your new job.

INDEX TO THE
QUESTIONS

The interviewers' questions

Are you a leader or a follower?   99

Are you ambitious?   100/137

Are you familiar with Total Quality Control? Do you use it currently?   144

Are you involved in writing procedures, specifications, tenders, etc in your current job?   119

Are you planning to continue your studies?   121

Are you reliable?   63

Are you sensitive to criticism?   77

Can you follow instructions?   89

Can you tell me more about how you fit into the organization? You work alone currently, don't you?   43

Can you tell me more about how you get the best out of your team?   42

Can you work under pressure?   117

Could you tell me more about [anything you've mentioned on your CV or application form]?   144

Describe a difficult customer you've had to deal with.   153

Describe a difficult decision you've had to make.   131

Describe a difficult problem you've had to deal with.   91/104/132/120/153

Describe a difficult sale you've made.   104

Describe a situation where your work was criticized. How did you respond?   77

Describe how your current job relates to the overall goals of your department or company.   111

Describe how your current job relates to the rest of the company.   154

Do you enjoy dealing with people?   150

Do you ever lose your temper?   103

Do you feel confident you would be able to do the job?   173

Do you feel you're overqualified/over-experienced for this position?   173

Do you feel your education prepared you for the workplace?   160

Do you feel your lack of experience could be a problem?   174

Do you feel your lack of qualifications could be a problem?   174

Do you get bored doing routine work?   63/88

Do you have more responsibilities now than when you started?   47

Do you like analytical tasks?   87/111

Do you like doing detailed work?   88

Do you like your current job?   186

Do you prefer routine tasks and regular hours?   89

Do you prefer working alone or with others?   48

Do you see yourself as a leader or a follower?   140

Do you think attention to detail is important in this sort of job?   186

Do you think speed or accuracy is the more important?   64/90

Do you work well under pressure?   90

Give me an outline of your current position.   41

Have you done the best work you're capable of doing?   79/120

Have you ever failed to meet a challenge?   78

Have you ever failed to reach your target?   103

Have you ever had any problems with supervisors?   62/86

Have you ever had to bend health and safety rules to get a job done?   65/115

Have you ever had to supervise people more qualified than you?   118

Have you ever worked under pressure? How did you cope with it?   163

Have you made any presentations in your current job?   120

Have you used MBO (management by objective) techniques before?   144

Have you worked without supervision?   84

Have you written any technical, procedural or training manuals for your company?   119

Have your responsibilities increased while you've been doing your current job?   47

How do you approach a project?   77/117

How do you behave under pressure?   152

How do you deal with criticism?   116

How do you deal with difficult decisions?   131

How do you deal with pressure?   102

How do you decide when it's appropriate to use your initiative or better to refer to your manager?   63

How do you decide when to use your initiative and when to refer to a supervisor/manager? 86

How do you define doing a good job in your profession? 113

How do you feel about routine work? 162

How do you feel about starting at the bottom? 162

How do you find out what your competitors are doing? 105

How do you get on with different types of people? 151

How do you get on with other people? 162

How do you get the best from people? 139

How do you go about making important decisions? 120

How do you go about recruiting a new member for the team? 145

How do you handle rejection? 78/102

How do you handle stress? 142

How do you handle tension? 102/152

How do you interact with people at different levels? 117/138

How do you keep aware of what's happening in other departments? 111

How do you keep up with changes/innovations in your profession? 72

How do you keep up with developments in your profession? 110

How do you keep up with what's happening in your field? 127

How do you make sure meetings run to time? 145

How do you manage/have you managed change? 128

How do you organize and plan for major projects? 145

How do you plan your workload? 104

How do you prioritize your workload? 142

How do you rate your confidence? 100

How do you react to stress? 152

How do you react when approached by someone who looks angry? 151

How do you respond to criticism? 133

How do you schedule your sales trips? 104

How do you work under pressure? 142

How has your job changed since you've been there? 46

How important do you think motivation skills are for a manager? 139

How long do you think it would take you to make a contribution? 144

How long do you think it would take you to make a contribution to this company? 99

How many footballs would it take to fill the lift you came up here in? 190

How many hours a week do you currently work? 142

How many hours a week would you say you work currently? 103

How well do you interact with people at different levels? 76

How well do you work in a team? 48

How well do you work without supervision? 60

How would you define a conducive working atmosphere?   129
How would you define your profession?   71/128
I notice that this job is rather different from your current/last one...   171
If you were a fruit or vegetable, what sort would you be?   191
Isn't this job a bit of a step backwards/sideways for you?   172
It's quite a long time since your last job...   171
Tell me about a difficult decision you had to make.   120
Tell me about a problem you've had to deal with.   64
Tell me about a time you had to persuade someone to do something they
    weren't keen to do.   154
Tell me about some of the projects you've worked on.   144
Tell me about yourself.   40
There are quite long gaps in your record. Is there a reason for that?   172
This job needs someone passionate about business improvement. Does
    that describe you?   101
This job needs someone who is passionate about business improvement. Is
    that you?   137
This position needs someone who is friendly and approachable. Is that how
    you would describe yourself?   150
Under what conditions do you work best/produce your best results?   75
We're offering around £00,000. How does that sound to you?   184
What appeals to you least about this job?   179
What are some of the problems you encounter in your current job?   153
What are some of the problems you encounter in your job?   64/91
What are the crucial aspects of your job?   113
What are the key factors for a successful team?   141
What are the main factors to consider when planning for growth?   144
What are the reasons for your professional success?   74
What are the reasons for your success in this profession?   98
What are the sorts of things colleagues do that really irritate you?   179
What are you like at influencing and persuading?   143/154
What are you like with deadlines?   79
What are you looking for in a job?   96/134/161/237
What are you seeking in an employer?   74
What are your best qualities?   59
What are your career plans?   173
What are your greatest accomplishments/achievements?   114/134
What are your greatest achievements?   74/96
What are your greatest strengths?   59/73/83/96/113/133/148/164
What are your outstanding qualities?   73/96/113/133/148

What are your qualifications for this job?   60/112

What are your views on customer service?   104/149

What are your views on health and safety?   65

What are your views on health and safety in your job?   115

What can you do for us that no one else can?   72/98/128

What conflicts do you anticipate between the needs of the shareholders and those of employees, and how would you balance them?   144

What did you dislike about your boss/supervisor?   179

What did you dislike about your last boss?   179

What did you learn from your last job?   47

What did you like about your weekend/holiday job/work placement?   160

What did you like least about your weekend/holiday job/work placement?   161

What does your current job entail? Describe a typical day to me.   42

What do you dislike about your current job?   179

What do you find most difficult about your current job?   182

What do you find most difficult to deal with in yourself?   181

What do you know about our company?   71/83/95/110/126/148

What do you regard as the essential skills for motivating people?   139

What do you see as the crucial aspects of your job/profession?   148

What do you think influences progress within a company?   164

What do you think is the key to successful negotiation?   104

What do you think makes a person approachable?   150

What do you think the key trends in the industry are?   96/110/127

What do you think you're worth?   185

What do you think you will find most difficult about this job?   182

What do you think your last boss could have done better?   179

What experience do you have for this job?   46

What has your current job taught you?   47

What have you been doing since your last job?   172

What have you done that shows initiative?   63/86/165

What have you learnt that you think would be useful here?   160

What interests you most about this job?   45

What is your approach to selling?   104

What is your attitude to challenge?   101/115/135

What is your attitude to risk?   76/101/115/135

What is your current salary?   184

What is your greatest weakness?   180

What kinds of decisions are most difficult for you?   131

What kinds of decisions do you make in your current job?   85

What kinds of decisions do you make independently in your current job? 62
What kinds of pressures arise in your job? 117
What kinds of pressures do you face in your current job? 143
What makes a good leader in your view? 140
What makes a good team member? 49
What makes a good... [what your job is]? 71
What makes you a good manager? 130
What makes you a good... [what your job is]? 60/83/98/112/148
What makes you think you'll be successful in this field? 161
What methods do you use to predict future workloads? 144
What motivates you? 134
What motivates you in your job? 105
What outside interests do/did you enjoy? 165
What qualities do you need to work unsupervised? 61/84
What skills do you feel are essential for team building? 141
What skills do you think are especially important when handling people tact-
    fully? 151
What software packages do you currently use for project manage-
    ment? 144
What sort of salary are you expecting? 183/185
What sort of things do you find difficult? 181
What sort of training methods do you use to develop your staff? 144
What's the biggest challenge you've faced? 101
What's the biggest mistake you've ever made in your job? 183
What type of appraisal systems do you use? 145
What type of training do you think is most effective? 144
What were your favourite subjects? 159
What were your reasons for leaving your last job? 49
What would you change about yourself if you could? 182
What would you do if a chatty colleague was interrupting your work? 91
What would you do if I told you your presentation earlier was terrible? 132
What would you do if someone on your team wasn't pulling their weight? 65
What would you do if we gave you a completely free hand? 72
What would you do if we gave you a free hand? 131
What would you do if your opinion differed from that of your boss? 118
What would you say are the reasons for your success? 133
What would you say makes a good... [what your job is]? 60
What would you say your attitude to challenge is? 75

When was the last time you felt angry?   103

When was the last time you got angry   152

When was the last time you lost your temper?   135

Where do you see yourself in five years' time?   164

Which aspects of the course interested you most?   159

Why did you choose the course/subjects you did?   159

Why do you believe you would make a good manager?   130

Why do you feel developing people is important?   139

Why do you think you would like this type of work?   161

Why do you want to change jobs?   49

Why do you want to work here?   44

Why should I hire you?   60/71/84/99/113/130

Would you call yourself a problem solver?   116

Would you describe yourself as a problem solver?   138

Would you object to being supervised by someone less qualified than you?   119

Would you say you follow instructions well?   62

Would you say you have authority?   137

Would you say you have good analytical skills?   111

Would you say you have good influencing skills?   99

Would you say you are confident?   136/151

Would you say you are determined?   100/138

Would you say you are innovative?   76/116/138

Would you say you are organized?   90

Would you say you are persuasive?   99

Would you say you are reliable?   87

You seem to have changed jobs frequently. Was there a reason for that?   170

You've been in your current job a rather short time. Why are you changing so soon?   170

You've had a wide range of different jobs...   171

You were in your last job a long time. How do you think you'd adjust to a new post?   169

You were in your last job for x years. Why weren't you promoted in that time?   170

Your last/current job seems a bit of a step down. Was there a reason for that?   172

Your questions for the interviewer

Do you promote internally?   194

How does the company see the job/department developing over the next few years?   195

How will you inform me of your decision – letter, phone, e-mail?   195

I'm very interested in this job and I believe I could do it well. May I ask if you have any reservations about my suitability?   195

If I were to join the company, where do you see me in five years' time?   194

What are the biggest challenges facing the team/department currently?   194

What are the company's current development plans?   195

What are the main priorities of this job over the next six months?   194

What would my career prospects be with the company?   194

When can I expect to hear from you?   195

Why has the job become vacant?   194

Index

NB: page numbers in *italic* indicate figures or tables

abilities, creative jobs 70
about yourself 40–41
accuracy, vs speed 64, 90
achievements
    college/school leavers 157
    creative jobs 70, 74
    management jobs 125, 134
    sales/marketing jobs 95, 96, 98
    technical jobs 114
adaptability 23–24, 35
administrative jobs 81–93
after the interview 227–35
ageism 173–74
ambition 100, 137–38, 169–70
analytical skills 87–88, 111
anecdotes 36
anger 103, 135, 152–53
anxiety 26
appearance 219–21
applying again 230
approachability 150
aptitude tests 211–13
assertiveness 118
assessment centres 202–03
attainment tests 207
authority 137

basic research 3–4
beginning the interview 38–43
behaviour
    at interview 221–23
    behavioural questions 52–56
benefits
    of job 45–46
    of you as an employee 13

best self, staying your 26–29
best work, your 79, 120
bigger picture, the 154
boredom 63, 88
breaks, taking 27
brevity 36
business journals 16–17
business learning tests 217

cardinal rules 36
career history
    creative jobs 69–70
    management jobs 125
    sales/marketing jobs 95
    technical jobs 109
career plans, your 173
case studies 208–09
challenge
    creative jobs 75–76
    management jobs 135–36
    sales/marketing jobs 101
    technical jobs 115
change management 128
character, your 190–91
choice of subjects 159–60
clerical jobs 81–93
closed questions 41–43,
        185–86
clothing 220–21
cognitive process profiling 217
college leavers 156–67
communication skills 117–20, 138–40,
        150–52
competencies 23, 34
    examples, giving 12–13

competitors, sales/marketing jobs 105–06
conducive working atmosphere 129–30
confidence 100, 136, 151, 173
contacting the company 3–4
continuing professional
    development 47–48
  college/school leavers 164
  creative jobs 72–73
  technical jobs 110, 121
contribution, making a 21, 99, 144
creative jobs 68–80
critical questions 177–83
criticism
  creative jobs 77–78
  current position 178–79
  management jobs 132–33
  technical jobs 116
  yourself 28–29, 179–83
crucial aspects of job 113, 148
cultural fit 21, 25, 44–45, 190–91
current position 41–43
  criticisms 178–79
  duration of 169–71
  internal communications 111
  learning from 47–48
  modification of 46–47
  overall goals 111
  reasons for leaving 49–51, 170–71
  responsibility 47
customer relations 146–55
customer service 104–05, 149
CVs, grading 4–5

daily timetable, your 27
deadlines, creative jobs 79
decision making 120–21, 131–32
defining your profession 71–72, 128
detail-oriented work 88
determination 100, 138
difficult questions 168–77
disabilities, questions about 175–76
documentation, creating 119

educational choices 159–60
efficiency 82
emails, sending 228–32
emotional intelligence tests 216
employability, demonstrating 25–26
employer's requirements 3–9
employment gaps 14–15, 171–72

engagement 21
essential questions 236–38
evidence
  competencies 11–14
  industry knowledge 16–19
  reassuring answers 14–15
  why you want the job 19
  your qualities 24–26
  yourself 40–41
exercise 28
experience 46
  clerical/administrative jobs 82–83
  college/school leavers 157
  customer relations 147–48
  lack of 174
  practical jobs 58
experience, lack of 174
explanations 14–15

favourite subjects 159
finish, the 5
first impressions 221–22
five years' time 164
flaws, your 179–83
freedom
  creative 72
  management jobs 131
frequent job changes 14–15, 170–71
friendliness 150

gaps in employment 14–15, 171–72
goals, setting 28
group exercises 209–10

health and safety 65, 115–16
hobbies, your 165–66
holiday jobs 160–61

illegal questions 175–76
impression, making an 31–35
inappropriate questions 175–76
inconsistent previous work 14–15
independence, practical jobs 62
industry knowledge 16–17
  management jobs 127
  sales/marketing jobs 96, 105–06
  technical jobs 110
influencing skills 99, 143, 154
informal interviews 203
initiative 63, 86–87, 165

innovation 72–73, 76, 116, 131, 138
instructions, following 62, 89
integrity 23, 35
intelligence 22, 33
interest in job 44–46
internal communications 111
interview structures 5
   future trends 205–18
   types of 197–204
interviewers 3–9
in-tray exercises 208

job description 7, 11
job hunting 26
job postings 11
job-replica exercises 208–09

keeping in contact 230
key skills
   clerical/administrative jobs 82
   college/school leavers 160–62
   creative jobs 70
   customer relations 147–48
   management jobs 125–26, 129–31
   practical jobs 58
   sales/marketing jobs 95
   technical jobs 109
know your enemy 3–9
knowledge of company 3–4, 21, 25,
   44–45
   clerical/administrative jobs 83
   creative jobs 71
   customer relations 148
   management jobs 126–27
   sales/marketing jobs 95
   technical jobs 110
knowledge of field 112–13

lasting impressions 223
leadership 99, 140–41
letters, sending 228–32
libraries 17
likeability 22–23, 32

management jobs 124–45
management skills 54
marketing jobs 94–107
mistakes made 53–54
modification of current position 46–47
more qualified persons 118–19

motivation 21, 44–46
   clerical/administrative jobs 84–85
   college/school leavers 161
   creative jobs 74–76
   management jobs 134–35, 139–40
   sales/marketing jobs 96, 105

negative questions 177–83
negotiation 104, 234
nerves, managing your 223–25
no offer made 228–33

off the wall questions 188–92
offers made 233–34
online tests 215–16
open questions 40–41
opinions, technical jobs 118
organizational skills 90
outside interests, your 165–66
over to you 5
overqualified, being 173–74

panel interviews 200–01
passion 101, 137
pay, questions about 183–85
people development 139
people, industry knowledge 17
people skills 54, 150–52
person specifications 7–9, 8
personality tests 214–15
personal qualities 21–26
person-specific questions 6
persuasiveness 99, 143, 154
physical tests 208
planning
   clerical/administrative jobs 90
   creative jobs 77
   management jobs 142
   presentations 207
   sales/marketing jobs 104
   technical jobs 117
portfolio, your 207
positivity 23, 33–34
practical jobs 57–67
practising, presenting evidence 14
preparation 10–20
presentation 219–26
   appearance 219–21
   behaviour 221–23
   nerves 223–25

presentations 120, 206–07
pressure
    clerical/administrative jobs 90
    college/school leavers 163
    customer relations 152–53
    management jobs 142–43
    sales/marketing jobs 102
    technical jobs 117
previous employment, wide-
    ranging 171
prioritization 142, 208
problem solving 189–90
    clerical/administrative jobs 91
    creative jobs 78
    customer relations 153
    management jobs 132, 138
    sales/marketing jobs 104
    technical jobs 116, 120
problems, handling 54
problems, practical jobs 64–65
procedures, technical jobs 119
productivity 129–30
professional development 47–48
    college/school leavers 164
    creative jobs 72–73
    technical jobs 110, 121
professional knowledge
    clerical/administrative jobs 92
    creative jobs 79–80
    customer relations 154
    management jobs 144–45
    practical jobs 66
    sales/marketing jobs 106
    technical jobs 121–22
profiling 210–17
projects, approach to 117
psychometric tests 210–11

qualifications 173–75
    college/school leavers 156
    practical jobs 60
    technical jobs 112
qualities 40–41
    clerical/administrative jobs 83–84
    college/school leavers 157, 161–62
    creative jobs 70–71, 73
    customer relations 147–49
    flaws 180–83
    management jobs 126, 128–31,
        133–34

off-the-wall questions 188–92
    practical jobs 59–61
    sales/marketing jobs 96–99
    standing out 21–30
    technical jobs 109, 113–14
questions 5
    answering 31–37
    behavioural 52–56
    structured 6, 44–51
    types of 6
    your questions to interviewers
        193–96

reasons for job change 49–51, 170–71
reassuring answers 14–15
rejection
    creative jobs 78
    of an offer 233
    and resilience 26
    sales/marketing jobs 102
reliability 58, 63–64, 87
repeat applications 230
resilience 26–29
responsibilities 47, 62, 85–86
risk, attitude to
    creative jobs 76
    management jobs 135–36
    sales/marketing jobs 101
    technical jobs 115
role playing 209
routine
    clerical/administrative jobs 88, 89
    college/school leavers 162

salary, questions about 183–85
sales jobs 94–107
school leavers 156–67
screening interviews 197–98
second interviews 203–04
self-care, practicing 26
selling, approach to 104
sequential interviews 201–02
serial interviews 201–02
sideways moves 172–73
speed, vs accuracy 64, 90
standard questions 6, 44–51
standing out 21–30
STAR strategy 53–55
starting at the bottom 162
starting the interview 38–43

step down, taking a 172–73
strengths
    college/school leavers 164–65
    creative jobs 73
    customer relations 148–49
    management jobs 133–34
    practical jobs 59
    sales/marketing jobs 96–98
    technical jobs 113–14
stress
    customer relations 152–53
    management jobs 142–43
    nerves, overcoming 223–25
structure of interviews 5
structured questions 6, 44–51
subject choices 159–60
successes, celebrating 29
supervision
    clerical/administrative jobs 86
    of more qualified persons 118–19
    technical jobs 118–19
    working without 60–62, 72, 84–85

tact 151–52
targets 103, 144
team building 141
teamwork 48–49
    clerical/administrative jobs 91–92
    college/school leavers 162–63
    creative jobs 76–77
    group exercises 209–10
    management jobs 138–39

practical jobs 65–66
    technical jobs 117–19
technical jobs 108–22
technical tests 207
technical writing 119
telephone interviews 198–99
temper, management jobs 135
tenders, technical jobs 119
tension 102, 152
trade publications 16–17
training manuals, creating 119
transferable skills 157–58, 160–61, 171
tricky questions 177–87
types of questions 6

unique capabilities, your 72, 98–99,
    128–29
unsupervised working 60–62, 72,
    84–85

video interviews 199–200
virtual reality tests 217
vision, management jobs 131

weaknesses, your 179–83
welcome, the 5
what you want in a job 161
why should I hire you 130
why you want the job 19
work experience 157, 160–61
work placements 160–61
working hours 103–04, 142

SECOND EDITION

ULTIMATE

PRESENTATIONS

MASTER INTERVIEWS
AND PRESENTATIONS TO
LAND YOUR DREAM JOB

JAY SURTI

FIFTH EDITION

ULTIMATE

CV

MASTER THE ART OF CREATING
A WINNING CV WITH OVER 100
SAMPLES TO HELP YOU GET THE JOB

MARTIN JOHN YATE

THIRD EDITION

ULTIMATE

IQ TESTS

1000 PRACTICE TEST QUESTIONS
TO BOOST YOUR BRAINPOWER

**KEN RUSSELL and
PHILIP CARTER**

FIFTH EDITION

ULTIMATE

**PSYCHOMETRIC
TESTS**

1000 QUESTIONS AND ANSWERS FOR VERBAL,
NUMERICAL, AND PERSONALITY TESTS

MIKE BRYON

FOURTH EDITION

ULTIMATE

APTITUDE TESTS

OVER 1000 PRACTICE QUESTIONS FOR
ABSTRACT VISUAL, NUMERICAL, VERBAL,
PHYSICAL, SPATIAL AND SYSTEMS TESTS

**JIM BARRETT and
TOM BARRETT**

FIFTH EDITION

ULTIMATE

COVER LETTERS

MASTER THE ART OF WRITING THE
PERFECT COVER LETTER TO BOOST
YOUR EMPLOYABILITY

MARTIN JOHN YATE

SIXTH EDITION

ULTIMATE

INTERVIEW

100s OF SAMPLE QUESTIONS AND
ANSWERS FOR INTERVIEW SUCCESS

LYNN WILLIAMS

SIXTH EDITION

ULTIMATE

JOB SEARCH

MASTER THE ART OF FINDING YOUR
IDEAL JOB, GETTING AN INTERVIEW
AND NETWORKING

LYNN WILLIAMS

FIND AND GET
THE JOB YOU WANT

KOGANPAGE.COM/ULTIMATE

CPSIA information can be obtained
at www.ICGtesting.com
Printed in the USA
LVHW071508311221
707636LV00030B/2484